Debt *IS* Slavery

Debt *IS* Slavery

Debt Free Living Is The First Step To Financial Freedom And Black Wealth Building

Dedicated to my Dad; Bobby J. Harris
Inspired by a conversation with Brother Thomas Jehad

Cover Graphics created by:
Creative Genius Technologies LLC
c/o Paul Muhammad
www.creativegeniustech.com
618-580-5548

Contents

PAY YOUR DEBTS

I do not and the Holy Qur-an and God Do Not Approve any Muslim as being a good Muslim, that goes and makes debts (whether it is with the Believers or Infidels) and then does not pay them. This is against the Law of Truth and Righteousness of Islam! Pay your debts or do not make them!!

**Elijah Muhammad,
Messenger of Allah**

Introduction

Let me begin with this disclaimer, I am not debt free (**YET**). Currently, I am in the middle of a 4-year plan and have thus far have eliminated well over $10,000 of debt in the years 2015 and 2016! As I continue the path that I am currently traveling to the destination of debt freedom, my scheduled finish line will be crossed July 2018.

This book includes some of the highs and lows of my 'debt free journey' along with details of the twists, turns and steps that this financial rollercoaster has taken me. Becoming debt free is a great emotional task! If was easier to spend the money than it has been to repay it. And I have found that writing this book is helpful on many levels as it is a reinforcement and somewhat of an accountability partner.

There are 3 parts of this book.

- **Articles** – The articles throughout the book will share data that details the current facts about American debt; who is in debt, what are the most common debts and how was the debt accumulated.
- **Charts** – Hands on activities that will help you to compile and understand your debt and look into your own financial mirror. For it to be effective, it is crucial that you are honest with yourself and the "numbers".
- **Tips** – These show you the steps to create a plan to get out of debt.

For the book to work for you, it is imperative that do more than read it. Use the articles as lessons in 'what **NOT** to do'. And you must complete the hands-on sections and apply what you are learning. Reading this book is not sufficient.

It is suggested that you read through the book one time. Let the facts and figures sink in. A few days later, come back a second time, reread and complete the hands-on sections. This will allow you to be a more informed and have a clearer vision of your finish line. You might be less emotional at this point too, because see yourself in the articles might be a little painful.

Lastly, if there is one theme throughout this book that you must take with you it is:

Becoming Debt Free Takes WORK!!!

You did not acquire your debt over night and chances are that you will not become debt free overnight. Even if you hit a lottery of several Millions, unless you learn and change your previous financial habits, you might soon find yourself back in debt. You must be realistic with your debt and its elimination. You can expect that it will take you months, but probably years to get out of debt So be willing and to give yourself some time. That 2-year plan that you initially develop might just take 3 years. Heck, my 3-year plan had to evolve as my life changed and now it is a 4-year plan. But its ok because my eyes are glued to my finish line. Become firm with yourself because this is serious business, but don't beat yourself down. If you fall off your become debt free horse, get back up – just don't fall off too many times. (smile)

Additionally, you must lose the attitude of **everybody has *debt**. Well, you are NOT everyone. And if you were not interested in becoming debt free or at least controlling your debt, you would not have purchased this book! *Note – I am speaking of an unmanageable debt.

My Debt Story
I recall watching my father every week, sitting at the dinner table paying bills. I was much younger and not yet responsible for bills, but I still could see that this activity brought him stress. I didn't really know what else to do, so I would come into the kitchen and without saying a word to him, stand next to him and place my hand on his ever-expanding oval shaped bald spot. I would stand there for about 30 seconds to a 1 minute with no verbal words exchanged. He would just sit still in acknowledgement that his child was trying to comfort him. I think my dad knew that I understood the stressfulness of debt.

So, if I grew up learning about the stress of debt, how did it happen to me. Easy, a series of events that ultimately cause me a downward spiral.

I always carried just a few credit cards; 4 or 5 of them. I was in the process of building a certain credit score so that at the appropriate time I would be able to purchase my own home. All total, the credit card limits were approximately $10,000 - $12,000. And my payments well in my salary. Well when my father passed, I realized that my retired mother needed financial help. And even though our home was paid for, Teaneck, NJ located in Bergen County is one of the most expensive places in the country live! Last time I looked, the county was the 36th wealthiest county in the nation. The house property taxes alone were nearly $10,000 a year. So, I made the decision that making sure that my mother was properly maintained was more important to me than maintain my own bills. I then I either paid the minimums on my debt or robbed Peter to pay Paul to make sure that my mother had whatever she needed.

For a period of time this worked well, as I self-employed working directly from home. I used to make jokes with my mother about being a 'kept' woman, she liked it and I was thrilled that I was making enough money to take care of her. When I finally got to the point that I was comfortably making enough money to maintain my mother, maintain the house and started to pay back my individual debts, tragedy struck, my mother transitioned. And she did so without a Will. So, you know the story. In came the vultures, oppps, I mean the siblings and off to probate court I went. When it was all said, and done, I had to sell my parents' home which essentially left both homeless and unemployed.

The maintainable amount of debt that I once had grew and grew and grew because I could no longer pay it. I then accumulated even more debt while struggling to survive and start a new life. So, that's the long story short of my debt story.

Now please know that I didn't share my story of how I accumulated debt to make anyone feel sorry for me, I'm just being transparent. Plus, if the truth be told, if I didn't go through what I went through, I would have never experienced what real debt looks and feels like. And this book **Debt *IS* Slavery** would not exist ☺ So now that you have heard MY story it's time for yours?

And now YOUR Journey Begins

How did you accumulate debt … Write it down, get it out of your system, believe me, you will feel better after you get the hurt, pain, anger and shame out.

_____
_____
_____
_____
_____
_____
_____
_____
_____
_____
_____
_____
_____
_____
_____
_____
_____
_____
_____

Scriptural References to Debt

Words of the Bible regarding Debt:

Proverbs 22:7 ESV
The rich rules over the poor, and the borrower is the slave of the lender.

Romans 13:8 ESV
Owe no one anything, except to love each other, for the one who loves another has fulfilled the law.

Psalm 37:21 ESV
The wicked borrows but does not pay back, but the righteous is generous and gives;

****

Holy Quran Words of Bible regarding debt:
O ye who believe! fulfil (all) obligations. 5:1

Words of the Hadith regarding debt:
"Whoever dies free from three things – arrogance, cheating and debt – will enter Paradise."

****

Words of the Talmud regarding debt:
Paying a creditor is a *mitzvah* [commandment][1]

---

[1] *Babylonian Talmud Ketubot 86a*

Words of the Wise Regarding Debt

The Honorable Minister Louis Farrakhan
You can't really be a man if you're in debt. I didn't have no debt. So don't put yourself in a position for someone to yank that chain.

Warren Buffet
Interest rates are very high on credit cards, … Sometimes they are 18%. Sometimes they are 20%. If I borrowed money at 18% or 20%, I'd be broke.

Dr. Boyce Watkins
Work your way out of debt.

Russian Proverb
Debt is beautiful only after it is repaid.

American Proverb
Before borrowing money from a friend, decide which you need most. –

Thomas Jefferson
Never spend your money before you have it.

Nathan W. Morris
Every time you borrow money, you're robbing your future self.

Prayers regarding Debt Removal

Refuge Prayer

'Oh ALLAH, I seek refuge in Thee from anxiety and grief. And I seek refuge in Thee from lack of strength and laziness. I seek refuge in Thee ALLAH from cowardice and niggardliness. And I seek refuge in Thee from being over-powered by debt and the oppression of men. Suffice Thou me with what is lawful, to keep away from me what is prohibited. And with Thy Grace, make me free of want from what is besides Thee.. Amen'

Debt Removal Prayer

Lord, I confess I've made mistakes. I have accumulated too much debt, and now I cannot imagine overcoming it without your help. Please Lord, I beg of you to intercede on my behalf. Provide me with the financial means to be able to breathe again. Please forgive my sins, Lord. Walk with me and help me to make the right decisions throughout my life. In your name I pray, Amen

Sacrifice

In becoming debt free, there are things that you are going to have to change and be willing to sacrifice. And the first thing that I think of when it comes to sacrifice is having to share one vehicle for nearly 3 years. The vehicle was a 15-year-old Ford Explorer. It was paid for in cash when it was purchased nearly 10 years ago, and ran well. (smile) On days that "Big Blue" was not available for me to drive, I walked, took public transportation or rode a bike! Yes, for one year, I rode a bike to the school that I taught at. Every time I rode up into the school's driveway the young students swarmed me as if I was a Rockstar showing up in a stretch limo. They though the bike was 'cool' My co-workers thought I was crazy. They all knew that I was working on becoming debt free, but felt the bike think was 'a bit much'.

Luckily for me, I am a vegetarian that loves simple foods so my sacrifice has included eating a great deal of beans and planning grocery trips to the dime. I'm talking, for several weeks, but food budget dropped down to $30 per week. I will talk more about this in the section "Meal Planning'.

Continuing with sacrifice, I let everyone know that I was working on becoming debt free. It didn't matter if I was on the bus, in the food market or talking to family, I found a way to include it in the conversation. There was a reason for this.

1. To make myself accountable.
2. Stopped people from asking to borrow money. **Nobody** would come and ask for
3. It's not in the Budget became ingrained in my everyday conversation. Whenever there was a fleeting thought to make an impromptu purchase, I verbally stated, It's not in the budget. Even if I was by myself, I said it out loud.

Another sacrifice was working 3 jobs. Yes, I said 3. I taught preschoolers, conducted covert customer service evaluations, and worked for Amazon in a fulfillment center. By the way, covert customer service evaluations is an upscale name for mystery shopping. When people thought, I was flying around the country taking 'vacations' I was actually flying out to locations to **WORK**!!!

My job at Amazon was to scan and "attach" packages to a pallet to be placed in an 18-wheeler and then shipped out. This means that I selected a box from a conveyor belt filled with packages, (I always picked small boxes), scan it, then located the corresponding pallet. I would then scan a package already located on the pallet, thus they would be 'attached'. I did this for 4 hours a day, 5 days a week for months. There were no chairs in the warehouse, and the work was nonstop. I kept a pedometer on my hip and by the end of any given shift, I would have walked anywhere from 1 ½ to 4 ½ miles.

I was remained focused and arrived everyday with a goal in mind. For example, when "Big Blue" began showing signs of death, I started making plans to secure a "new to me" vehicle; a 2013 certified pre-owned 535i BMW. Poverty is not my friend, I believe in wisely being upscale. Anyway, I had not had a car payment in over a decade and working on becoming debt free did not include a car payment but I knew that I didn't have that type of cash, so I created a plan that would allow me to purchase a 2009 535i BMW first. I would keep that for 6 to 12 months, continue working an extra job or two and save until I had enough to purchase the 2011 version, using a trade in of the 2009 of course. And when that phase was completed, I would then focus my efforts on the 2013 model. So, with every scan I would state some type of positive affirmation to remind myself of the goal.

Scan – Paying cash for my "new to me car."
Scan – BMW
Scan – 535i
Scan – Certified Preowned
Scan – Sunroof
Scan – Beige Leather Seats
Scan – Heated seats
Scan – Positive Affirmation, Positive Affirmation, Positive Affirmation,

I have not had cable television in nearly 8 years. I have streamed and now use SlingTV.

The Average American Pays This Amount For Cable, How Do You Compare?
Do you pay more or less for pay-TV than the average American?

In the past 70 years, it can be argued there's no product that's changed America quite like the television set. From an estimated 6,000 sets in use in 1946 to nearly three televisions per household now, television has grown from luxury to ubiquity in less than three generations. It is now estimated the average American over age two watches roughly five hours of television per day -- 34 hours per week.

The rise of cable television enabled this rapid growth. Initially designed to improve reception for homes unable to receive over-the-air signals, by a system of antennas and coaxial cable delivery, cable television later expanded to include new programming networks and services. As a result, both the number of subscribers and programming choices exploded. As a matter of fact, the broader subscription pay-TV market in the U.S. is estimated at more than 100 million with the average customer now having 189 channels .

But programming choices, quality, and subscriber counts aren't the only thing that's exploded -- so has the average cable bill. According to estimates from the NPD Group, this year the average subscription pay-TV customer will pay an astonishing $123 per month for pay-TV. NPD estimated that same figure was $86 in 2011, which indicates an increase of 9.4% annually between 2011 and 2015.

For perspective, total U.S. inflation as measured by the Consumer Price Index increased 1.6% annually during that period, leading many to question the sustainability of a business model that's charging subscribers roughly six times the rate of inflation annually.

Pity the poor pay-TV provider

*In an ironic twist, pay-TV providers -- **Comcast**, **Time Warner Cable**, and **DirecTV**, among others -- aren't the underlying cause for your exploding bill. Both the Federal Communications Commission and media-insights firm SNL Kagan point toward programming costs as the main reason for the increase. And that makes sense, as the costs of ESPN, TNT, and Fox News increase, your cable bill will increase to pay for sports, original programming, and political-focused punditry.*

Lost in the thank you is the fact you'll be paying 50% more for the channel. Source: Dish

*For example, **Dish Network** and Fox News recently settled programming dispute that led to Fox News being removed from Dish's channel lineup. After a near-month hiatus, the dispute was resolved with Fox News receiving a 50% increase for the cost of content. Bringing in SNL Kagan's earlier estimates of Fox News averaging nearly $1 per subscriber monthly pre-dispute, eventually a $0.50 per month increase (plus Dish's profit margin) will need to be paid by subscribers. And that's only one channel out of nearly 200.*

Want a friend in Washington? Get a dog

Adding more irony to the situation, one of the strongest moves that Comcast and Time Warner Cable have to combat content cost increases for subscribers may be denied due to prior poor subscriber treatment. The proposed Comcast-Time Warner Cable merger would create a massive entity boasting roughly one-third of all subscription TV subscribers. With that scale comes the ability to negotiate more effectively with channels to lower content costs or to slow its rapid growth.

The Stop Mega Comcast Coalition continues to pick up steam. Source: Stop Mega Comcast

However, due to years of perceived poor customer service, Comcast and Time Warner find themselves facing a tougher battle than expected with the L.A. Times no longer viewing the merger as "inevitable." The merger review period was recently paused for a second time by the FCC due to what FCC Media Bureau Chief William Lake called substantial and material errors.

Regardless of Washington's decision, customers are voting with their wallets

*And while it is hard to know where the political winds of Washington will blow, many consumers are voting with their wallets. In 2013, the number of pay-TV subscribers actually fell as more are embracing streaming-based services like **Netflix** and **Amazon.com** Prime Video. Last year, Experian Marketing found 6.5% of U.S. households have cut the cord -- up from 4.5% in 2010.*

And while it is important to note this trend is still small, it is increasing. Recently, Dish Network unveiled its Sling live-streaming service in an attempt to monetize this trend. One thing's for sure, if the industry thinks it can continue to raise prices at six times the rate of inflation, this trend of cord cutting will only continue.[2]

---

[2]http://www.fool.com/investing/general/2015/02/01/the-average-american-pays-this-amount-for-cable-ho.aspx

Teamwork

If you are married, you and your spouse **MUST** be on the same page or becoming debt free will be 10 times harder. You will need help and encouragement. This is not negotiable because clearing debt is an emotional rollercoaster. There will be days when you are down an will be in need of a pick me up word from your spouse and vice versa. So … gotta get your spouse onboard. So if you are single, you should locate friends, your accountability partners, that well help you to stay on target.

Accountability Partners

During the spring of 2016, I was traveling out of state with a childhood friend. We decided to take a visit to a luxury retail store. Initially, we went our separate ways in the store, as she was looking for a coat and I wanted to check out the handbags.
And then I found it, a beautiful black leather luxury hand bag. It was large enough to hold all of my daily belongings, and it was on sale for **ONLY** $219. It was 50% off. I touched it. I smelled it. I modeled it in front of the mirror and then I ran through the store to locate my friend so that I could show her the bag. And she kinda just looked at me when I told her about the handbag but agreed to come look at it anyway.

When we both arrived in the handbag section, I caressed the bag, and encouraged her to do the same, making statements such as, "look, it's on sale" and "it feels like butter right?" Well, after watching me act like a fanatic over this bag, she finally stated, "Yeah, it's nice, but is it in your budget?" After looking at her in silence for about 10 seconds, she walked away, leaving me alone with the handbag to say goodbye to it

She knew about my debt free journey and would not co-sign on my foolish spending. I was so upset with her at that moment, thinking thoughts like, "she is not really my friend" and "she just doesn't want to me to have this nice handbag." But looking at it now, she showed me that she was a GREAT friend for not 'going there' with me.

Spending Habits

The Joneses, Muhammad's and Rodriquez'

We all know them, the Jones', the Muhammad's and the Rodriquez'. They live in nice homes with big screen televisions in every room. They drive the latest model cars and are always raving about what they have. But they don't tell their little secret, which is **THEY ARE BROKE**.

- The Joneses have a $500 a month car payment for 6 years.
- The Muhammad's are underwater with their house, which they secured with a sub-prime lender – because they had bad credit.
- The Rodriquez's have 50k in credit card debt and 75k in student loans.

They are living paycheck to paycheck and stay nervous about not losing their job. If you resemble any of these families, have no fear. In the section you will learn how to make this a thing of the past.

That New Car

When I see nice new cars, I don't marvel and think, OMG, that car looks amazing, what I see is a car payment.

Growing up, I learned from my parents that it is best to drive a car that you can afford and ideal if you can pay cash for your car. Only once did I see my parents purchase a brand-new car. My father drove that car into the ground and knowing him, it was probably paid off well in advance of the scheduled paid in full date.

Going against what I had been taught by example, I once purchased a brand-new vehicle. It was a 2002 White Chrysler Sebring. I remember pulling up in my parents driveway and my father, with a frown on his face, pointing at the sparkling new car and saying "What's this?" He knew I didn't have the cash to pay for the vehicle outright, so I must have taken a loan out for its purchase. He never once wrote in that car!

Well, let's fast forward in time. Six months after receiving the title, someone crashed into it and totaled it. Yes, 48 payments of $325.81 per month and POOF, it was GONE. I was compensated with a $5000 check from my insurance company. That was my first and last time buying a brand-new car. Now I save my money and purchase used cars with cash. I have learned that this is a common practice of millionaires by reading the book, *The Millionaire Next Door* written by Thomas J. Stanley.

Americans set record for auto loans.

Americans are paying more every month for a new vehicle and making those payments for a longer time than ever.

The latest data on auto loans by Experian shows Americans are taking out record-size loans, making larger monthly payments than ever before and extending their loans farther than ever.

The numbers from millions of auto loans tracked in the first quarter of this year are striking.

Average auto loan: $30,032 — the first time the amount borrowed to buy a new vehicle has topped $30,000.

New car, new reality; Auto loan borrowing hits fresh highs

Average monthly payment: $503 — the first time the average auto payment has gone over the $500 mark.

Average term for an auto loan: 68 months — this is the longest average term ever seen by Experian.

"This is kind of the natural evolution we would expect in conjunction with vehicles costing more," said Melinda Zabritski, Experian's senior product director of automotive finance. Experian tracks millions of auto loans, which totaled more than $1 trillion in value in the first quarter.

Auto loans and payments have been growing steadily over the past seven years as the price of new vehicles has climbed. TrueCar said the average transaction price for a new vehicle hit $32,994 in May, up 3.4 percent on the same month a year ago.

What's noteworthy about Experian's report is the data that show consumers are adjusting to the reality of what it costs to buy a new vehicle.

For example, loan payments topping $500 is significant because consumers have long expressed a desire to keep their monthly bill under $500 if possible. It's the reason leasing, where the average monthly payment was $406 in the first quarter, has become more popular in recent years.

"Five-hundred dollar monthly payments could change the psychology for [the] auto buyer," Zabritski said. "Buyers want that monthly payment as low as possible."

That's the reason consumers are stretching out auto loans farther than ever to a new record of 68 months. The longer the term, the lower the monthly payment. In the first quarter, almost a third of all auto loans came with repayment terms of 73-84 months, which was the most popular term among new vehicle buyers.

Zabritski says the growth in auto loans is worth watching to make sure consumers don't wind up going "upside down" on auto loans, but she feels the auto loan market is generally healthy.[3]

Like I mentioned earlier, I will never again purchase a brand-new car, instead I save up for my cars and then use it to obtain a better one. Below is an overview of what I am currently doing to purchase my "new to me" BMW 535i.

When it comes to money, normal is broke. You want to be weird, and weird people don't have car payments.

So how, exactly, do you live without a car payment?

Here's the deal. Recent statistics show that one-third of car buyers sign up for a six-year loan at an average interest rate of 9.6%. Among these buyers, the average price of the car is just over $26,000. This means that one-third of the cars you see on the road are dragging a $475 payment behind them.

---

[3] Http://www.cnbc.com/2016/06/02/us-borrowers-are-paying-more-and-for-longer-on-their-auto-loas.html

The car dealer won't tell you that your awesome new car loses about 25% of its value the instant you drive it off the lot. After four years, your car has lost about 70% of its value! What does that mean? After six years, you've paid almost $33,000 for a $26,000 car, which is now worth maybe $6,000. Not a good deal.

Here's a new plan. What if you bought a cheap $2,000 car just to get around for 10 months? Then you take that $475—the average car payment—save it every month, and pay for a new car (with cash!), instead of giving it to the bank.

After 10 months of doing that, you'll have $4,750 to use for that new ride. Add that to the $1,500–2,000 you can get for your old beater, and you have well over $6,000. That's a major upgrade in car in just 10 months—without owing the bank a dime![4]

[4] http://www.daveramsey.com/blog/the-truth-about-car-payments

Rent A Center and Payday Loans

When I hear the names of these businesses', the word scam comes to mind. Plain and simple, these businesses are a scam. They aren't located or marketed in so-called White or affluent communities. They however, target urban and low income neighborhoods; mostly where many of the population have poor credit. The following article written by Ryan Mack gives examples of how these companies operate and make money from the poor.

	Regular Sofa and Love Seat	Leather Sofa and Love Seat	26 Inch Sony Bravio TV	52 Inch Sony Bravio TV
Weekly Payment	$19.99	$30.99	$17.99	$59.99
Retail Value	$900	$2,000	$550	$1900
Weeks Until You Own from Rent-A-Center	78	78	104	116
Interest Rate	80%	26%	163%	159%
Interest Paid	$659	$417	$1,321	$5,059
Total Paid	$1,559 for a $900 Sofa	$2,417 for a $2000 Sofa	$1,871 for a $550 Television	$6,959 for a $1,900 Television

As you can see from the chart there is a clear disadvantage from those who choose the Rent-A-Center way versus those who choose to be prudent about how they purchase items for their house. If you take the 52-inch Sony Bravio television, which retails for $1900, one could use the $59.99 that he/she would be giving to RAC to purchase the product and putting it into a savings account. Doing it the smart way would allow you to purchase this TV in just 31 weeks. However, through RAC you would be paying on that TV for a total of 116 weeks before you actually own it. Over that time period you would pay a total of $6,959. When you subtract the total paid ($6,959) from the retail value of the TV ($1900) I calculated that you would have *paid over $5000 in interest at a rate of 159%. Being prudent saves you 85 weeks of payments and over $5000 that you could have used to put towards retirement, a new home, a business, or another more meaningful use. Doing it the smart way you could almost purchase 4 TVs of an equivalent price in the time that it takes you to purchase just one TV doing it the RAC way.[5]*

MY PAYDAY LOAN EXPERIENCE .....

Yes … I once was in situation that I felt was so desperate that not only did I consider taking out I payday loan, I actually followed through and secured one. My loan was $350.00 and I loved payday loans on the day that I received the money. But the love affair quickly went sour. The terms of the loan were that I was to pay $75.00 each week until the loan was paid off. Well, the first week was fine and the second week was a little struggle, but by the three week, my finances were 'off' again and I could not pay. Ok, I am not going to lie, after that week 3, I fanned my hand and stated, "I'm not paying these damn people." So, I didn't, for two years. However, when my financial situation became more stable, I reached out to the company and informed that I that I wanted to settle this debt. Below, you can read my communications with the pay day loan company word for word:

Landra to the Creditor: Dear Sir / Madam I would like to settle this debt. I can pay $25 per month or settle in full for $400. Thank You in advance for your assistance.
Creditor to Landra: Hi Landra, Thank you for contacting us. It's great to hear that you can start making payments towards this balance. The link below will show your personal payment plan that I have customized to fit your needs, at just $43.75 per month. Take a look: Your Personal Payment Plan You can get this set up as soon as possible, but you will not be charged until May 6, so make sure to sign up today. Please don't hesitate to contact us if there is anything else we can do for you. I'll check in with you in a few days to help answer any questions.
Landra to the Creditor: Thank you for your response. My budget allows for me to pay $25 per month, or I can settle this bill for $400.00 Thank you for your assistance.

---

[5] http:newsone.com/872335/the-scam-that-is-rent-a-center/

Creditor to Landra: Hi Landra, Thanks for letting us know. We can settle the balance for $400. Would you be able to pay the entire sum at once? If so, when?

Landra to the Creditor: The $400.00 settlement will be paid in two payments, May 15, 2016 and June 15, 2016. Please feel free to email me this paid as agreed settlement plan at my current email address. Thank you for your assistance.

Landra to the Creditor: Thank you. I have just taken a look at the webpage of the payment set up for two payments of $200.00. Now please e-mail me documentation that this bill will be settled for $400.00 Please use my current email address to send the paid as agreed settlement plan. Thank you.

Creditor to Landra: Hi Landra, You will receive a confirmation email once the settlement of $400 has been paid in full using the link provided for the customized payment plan in the last email. Please let me know if I can further assist in signing you up.

Landra to the Creditor: To participate in a payment plan, the terms of the settlement agreement need to emailed to me in advance. I thank you for your assistance.

Creditor to Landra: Hi Landra, Per your request, please see the settlement offer letter attached. Your payment link can be accessed here: Your Personal Payment Plan Please let me know if you have any questions in getting set up.

Hopefully, that was that transparent enough for you? When I showed a close friend the dialog and told her that I was going to include it in the book, she looked perplexed and asked was I sure that I wanted to share that much information. I chuckled and let her know that it was important to let others know that they are not alone managing debt. Notice how firm I was. Read more about the steps to creating a settlement in the section: "Settlements."

Weaves, Nails and Designer Bags

During my research for this book, I came across a statistic that was quite disturbing. There must have been some mistake, because there was no way possible that Black women have a net worth of $5. **ONLY FIVE DOLLARS**? However, as I continued to research, I realized that the statistic was correct and proved to be an inspiration to finish writing this book.

STUDY: Single Women of Color Age 36-49 Have Median Wealth Of Just $5

According to a report released by the Insight Center for Community Economic Development this week, there is a vast discrepancy in wealth between single women of color and single white women.

The study, "Lifting As We Climb: Women of Color, Wealth, and America's Future," found that while the median net worth of single white women ages 36-49 is $42,600 — 61 percent of the median wealth for same-aged, single white men — single women of color in the same age group have a median wealth of just $5.

Black and Hispanic women are also drastically worse off in a broader age bracket, with almost half of single black and single Hispanic women ages 18-64 reporting zero or negative wealth (46 percent and 45 percent, respectively), compared with 23 percent of single white women, according to the report.
The financial situations of single women of color are so precarious, the study found, that just one unpaid sick day or appliance repair would send about half of them into debt.

And while marriage appears to ameliorate some economic hardship for both men and women across races, the data indicate that the positive effect of marriage on net worth is particularly amplified for black and Hispanic women.

The report offers a number of possible explanations for the wealth gap, including prior and current institutional factors (such as wage disparities and access to fringe benefits in the workplace), as well as a higher rate of being targeted by predatory lenders. (A recent study by the National Council of Negro Women and the National Community Reinvestment Coalition, the authors point out, found that across income groups, black and Hispanic women were much more likely to be caught up in expensive loans than white women.)

But a number of policies, the authors argue — enhanced employment opportunities, support for self-employment and microenterprise, incentives to save and stronger social insurance — would go a long way toward closing the wealth chasm:

"It is the author's intent and sincere hope that shining a spotlight on women of color and wealth becomes a catalyst for policy change - change that will lift women of color as they continue their climb toward economic security. Their futures are inextricably linked with the economic future of the nation.[6]

So, this article inspired me to discover where Black Women's money was going, and loe and behold, I ran across this information. We wear it on our heads, on our arms in the form of handbags and on our fingernails.

Weave – A multi-billion dollar industry

One's hair is a form of self-expression and over the years individuals—females and to an extent males—have invested billions into the hair extension industry. Females of different races and ethnicities wear hair extensions, more popularly called weave, for different reasons including to achieve length, protection and boost confidence.

According to the 16th annual "Buying Power of Black America" Report published by Target Market News, a leading group focused on African-American marketing, advertising and media, African-Americans spent $507 billion of their estimated buying power of $836 billion on hair care and personal grooming items in 2009. That's a $72 billion dollar difference from that spent in 2008.

While weaves can range in prices from $20 to $10,000 USD, it is no surprise that it is a multi-billion-dollar lucrative business. Weaves also are sold in varying lengths, colors and textures to suit the specifications of the buyer.[7]

And just so that nobody thinks I that I am singling out Black Women – Black Men, you have helped to make Michael Jordan a Billionaire by wearing

---

[6] http://www.huffingtonpost.com/2010/03/11/women-of-color-have-media_n_495238.html
[7] https://thecaribbeancurrent.com/weave-a-multi-billion-dollar-industry/

sneakers! The statistics were so horrific that I didn't want to include them in the book, but I listed them anyway.

The Jordan brand remains a cash cow for its owner NIKE (NKE) and its namesake MJ. The overall U.S. basketball shoe market was up 3.7% in 2015, while the Jordan brand's growth was almost four times that at 14% according to research firm SportsOneSource. The Jordan business is split almost evenly between the retro product and new releases. Total Jordan U.S. retail shoe sales hit $3 billion last year with a market share of 64% in basketball compared to 29% for Nike-proper, 3.6% for Under Armour (US) and 2.3% for Adidas per SportsOneSource. His Nike deal was worth $100 million for MJ last year, by our count, or more than the $94 million in total playing salary he made during 15 NBA seasons.[8]

---

[8] http://www.forbes.com/sites/kurtbadenhausen/2016/03/30/how-michael-jordan-will-make-more-than-any-other-athlete-in-the-world-this-year/#404fa4db5044

Wealth Behavior versus Poverty Behaviors

I am blessed that I learned at a young age that people that 'looked' like they had, probably didn't, and the people that looked regular, well, that was where the real money was. The following article shows this to be true.

Wealthy People Make Different Choices With Their Money Than The Rest Of Us

Everyone doesn't spend the same.

Building wealth and achieving financial independence is like losing weight or quitting smoking. It is simple, but not easy.

The first requirement of building wealth is to know the difference between assets and liabilities. Assets put money into your wallet, preferably each month. They will feed you even if you are not working. Examples of assets include income-generating real estate, dividend-paying stocks and interest-paying bonds.

As an asset class, investment real estate has the advantage of providing rental income, appreciation and other tax advantages.

Liabilities take money out of your wallet, usually monthly. They will eat your income even if you are working. The most common liabilities are credit cards with outstanding balances, consumer loans, home equity lines of credit, and home mortgages.
That is correct: Your home mortgage is actually a liability to you and an asset to the mortgage holder, since it takes money out of your wallet and puts it into the bank's pocket every 30 days. If you were to lose your job, this liability would be the one that would eat your savings the fastest.

Everyone has expenses. What characterizes poor households is that almost all of their earned income flows into the Expense Box (Fig. 1).

Fig. 1-1 Cash Flow Path of Poor Households

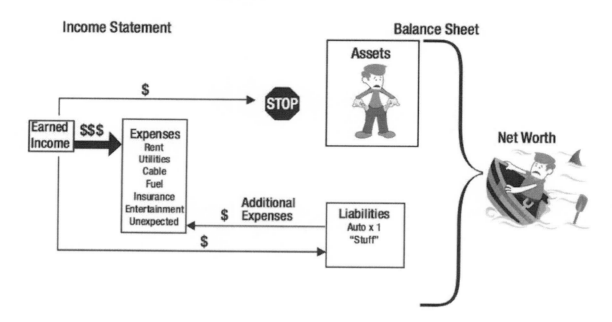

They struggle just to maintain a roof over their heads, food on the table, and a car in the driveway. They have just a little money to put into their Liability Box and no money for the Asset Box.

Rich and middle class households share similar cash flow patterns. Again, everyone has the basic living expenses in the Expense Box, and the middle class and rich households have proportionately higher living expenses than the poor households.
Rich people are often the successful professionals in the community and are characterized as having high-earned incomes, but usually they also have expensive lifestyles with a lot of "stuff"

in their Liability Box. Although they are high earners, they often live paycheck to paycheck. Most of their cash flows from the Earned Income Box down to the Liability Box (Fig. 2).

Fig. 1-2 Cash Flow Path of Middle Class / "Rich" Households

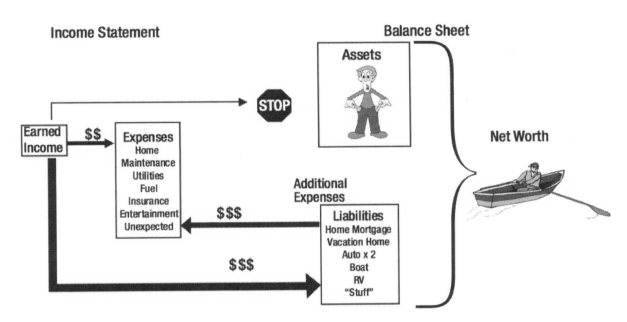

But the defining characteristic is the huge amount of "stuff" in the Liability Box, which drains a disproportionately high percentage of the earned income to both buy and support those liabilities.

The second characteristic that you will notice is that, much like the poor households, neither the middle class nor the rich have money flowing into the Asset Box to generate passive income.

This is a tragic domestic cash flow. Unlike the poor, the middle class and rich do have options available to them, but every time they pull out their credit card or checkbook they just keep choosing the wrong options ... they choose to put their earned money into liabilities instead of assets.

Fig. 1-3 Cash Flow Path of Wealthy Households

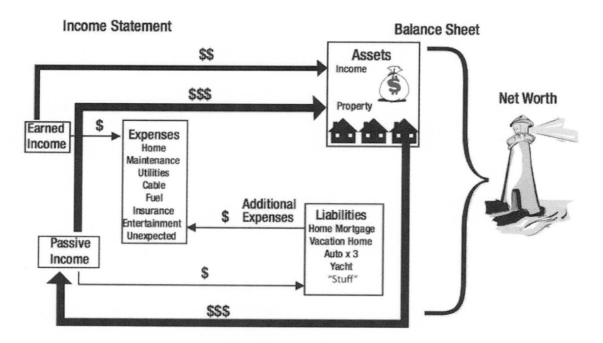

As shown in Fig. 3, the wealthy households have an Asset Box and you now see a flow of earned income into the Asset Box. So not only do wealthy households have more money flowing out of the Earned Income Box, but more importantly, they now have additional, passive income being

generated in the Asset Box. Although they have more "stuff" in their Liability Box, the wealthy use their passive income rather than their earned income to support these liabilities.

Unlike the poor, middle class or rich, the wealthy households have income generators in the Asset Box, which generate passive income that can now support the living expenses, the Liability Box and, most importantly, flow back into the Asset Box to buy new income-generating assets to continuously build wealth.

What separates the wealthy from the poor, middle class and rich is this automatic feedback loop between the Asset Box and the Passive Income Box. At some level this feedback loop becomes self-sustaining, the Earned Income Box becomes unnecessary, and the household becomes truly financially independent.

So the next time you are considering buying something that will just add more "stuff" to your Liability Box, consider putting your hard earned money to work instead by using it as a down payment to invest in, for example:

- Compact rental houses
- Well-located duplexes
- Small office/warehouse industrial rental units
- Workforce or retiree mobile home parks

Your tenant's rent should be covering the utilities, property taxes and insurance, along with paying down the mortgage, leaving you with money left over to put towards your next income producing asset.

Soon your Liability Box will be shrinking, your Asset Box will be growing and you will be building wealth and on the road to financial independence.[9]

---

[9] http://www.businessinsider.com/how-cash-flows-2015-1

The previous section provided a great deal of information, so just to make sure that you understand the difference between **Assets** and **Liabilities**, list the following under the appropriate column. The answers can be found in the acknowledgments section.

Jordan Sneakers	Artwork	Credit Cards	Mutual Funds	BMW 535i
Land	Checking Account	Jewelry & Furs	House	Student Loan

Assets	Liabilities

Now that you have a better understanding of Assets and Liabilities, take note of your personal belongings and list yours.

Assets	Liabilities

Personal Notes:

_____
_____
_____
_____
_____
_____
_____

Before you start tackling your debt ... Rainy Day Fund

Ok, you have read a ton of statistics. You may have even seen yourself in the previous articles, so at this point you should be excited and ready to start this Debt Free Journey; however, there is something that must be done first. You must begin with creating a Rainy-Day Fund also known as an Emergency Fund.

What Is An Emergency

An emergency fund is a stash of money set aside to cover the financial surprises life throws your way. These unexpected events can be stressful and *costly.*[10]

Examples of Emergencies include:
- Job losses
- Medical or dental emergencies
- Major home repairs that cannot be put off (e.g., damage due to a natural disaster, a leaking roof)
- Major car repairs
- Bereavement-related expenses for loved ones

Just a note – A WANT is NOT an emergency. An emergency is ALWAYS a NEED.

Initially, you might think, well if I am already in debt and currently struggling to pay my bills to start with, so how in the world am I going to establish an emergency fund. Well, to be honest, it's going to take extra work on your part. You are going to work harder. Both planning and probably some physical work as well.

---

[10] https://investor.vanguard.com/emergency-fund/

63% Of Americans Don't Have Enough Savings To Cover A $500 Emergency

The car brakes go on the fritz. The refrigerator stops refrigerating. The dog gets his paws on a batch of chocolate chip cookies and earns himself a trip to the vet ER.
These are just three of any number of things that could go wrong during the course of the year. Recovering from any one will set you back about $500, which means these scenarios fall closer to the "undesirable inconvenience" category than they do the "massive calamity" one. And yet, nearly two-thirds of Americans do not have enough money in savings to cover the cost of a single one of these unplanned expenses.

According to a brand-new survey from Bankrate.com, just 37% of Americans have enough savings to pay for a $500 or $1,000 emergency. The other 63% would have to resort to measures like cutting back spending in other areas (23%), charging to a credit card (15%) or borrowing funds from friends and family (15%) in order to meet the cost of the unexpected event.

It's not news that Americans are terrible savers. In November, Pew Charitable Trusts reported that one in three American families have no savings at all. In December, Magnify Money released the results of a study that found that 56.3% of people have less than $1,000 in their checking and savings accounts combined. Sensing a trend? You should: America's saving struggle has been a problem year after year after year.

But this latest survey is particularly striking because of the implications it carries.
"Five-hundred dollars is enough money that it could be catastrophic if you're really living on the edge and don't have enough money" to cover that unplanned cost, Bankrate senior investing analyst Sheyna Steiner said in a phone interview. "I did wonder what would happen if it was $10,000, what would the answer have been then?"

A $10,000 emergency is a somewhat rare occurrence for families of moderate income — but it's hardly unheard of. According to the Pew Charitable Trusts analysis, the median size of a family's most expensive financial "shock" (as they call it) in a year is $2,000. But Pew also found that the cost of emergencies actually varies by income: for households with an income *of $25,000 or less, the median cost of the most expensive financial shock is $1,000, a figure that equates to 31 days' worth of income. As you move up the income spectrum, the median cost of unplanned expenses goes up, but the days' worth of income necessary to pay for that expense goes down. So for families making between $50,000 and $85,000, for instance, the median financial shock was $2,500 — or 13 days' worth of income. Families who reported $85,000 or more in household income were the ones most likely to see that $10,000 emergency, 26 days' worth of income:*

Figure 2

The Median Household's Most Expensive Shock Cost Higher-Income Households More but Was a Greater Burden on Lower-Income Households

Cost distribution for the most expensive shocks, in days of income and dollars

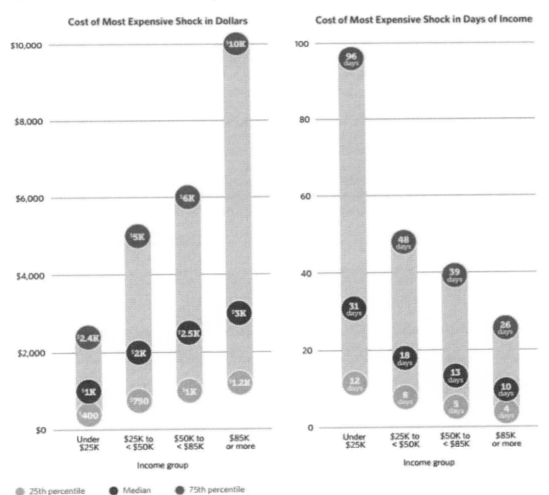

Cost of Most Expensive Shock in Dollars

Cost of Most Expensive Shock in Days of Income

25th percentile   ● Median   ● 75th percentile

Source: Survey of American Family Finances by Pew Charitable Trusts.

But that's the median size of a household's most expensive financial emergency. (How's that for a brain twister? Not the median cost of a financial emergency, but the median size of the most expensive financial emergency in a year.) Zooming out and looking at the most typical types of unplanned expenses that a family can experience throughout a year, Pew found that the most common was a car repair — which puts us back in the $500 to $1,000 realm that Bankrate used in its queries. The one that just 37% of people said they'd pay for using savings. If all of the above sounds like doom and gloom, there is a bit of a silver lining here: 23% of Bankrate respondents said they'd pay for a $500 or $1,000 emergency by cutting back on non-essential spending, like eating out at restaurants and buying coffee from a coffee shop rather than home brewing. This indicates that there's a bit of elasticity in people's budgets.
Steiner also noted that it is encouraging that people appear more likely to scrimp on other spending before resorting to the use of a credit card in the face of an unplanned event.

"It was striking that so few people would just immediately put it on their credit card," she said. "But if you've got a little wiggle room, maybe [a $500 unplanned expense] is just low enough that you could maybe lower your spending."[11]

---

[11] http://www.forbes.com/sites/maggiemcgrath/2016/01/06/63-of-americans-dont-have-enough-savings-to-cover-a-500-emergency/#78b28e606dde

Where Do I Get the Money

You are going to change certain old habits and create new ones. You are also going to work more. Meaning in addition to whatever work you are already doing. It's just that simple. It's not for the rest of your life that you will have to do this, but you have to make a change now if you want to see a change in your financial future.

Ways to Get Your Emergency Fund Started

Request a rate reduction on your credit cards

If you're carrying a credit card balance, getting your interest rate reduced will directly save you money each month. Just flip over your credit card, call the number on the back, ask to speak to a supervisor, and simply request that the rate be reduced. Suggest that you're considering transferring your balance off of the card.
Shop around for better auto insurance and homeowner's insurance

Install a programmable thermostat – and program it

Pretty simple, actually – it just takes thirty minutes or so and will cut your cooling and heating bill by 20 or 30 percent. Set it so that the air conditioner and/or furnace don't run while you're sleeping or at work so that the energy isn't wasted when no one is around or awake to enjoy it.

Use a list for grocery shopping

Ten minutes of planning before you go will save you at least ten minutes in the store, plus it will help you stay focused on the stuff you actually need, reducing your grocery bill because you're putting less unnecessary stuff in the cart. (See chapter XX for more on (Meal planning)

Transform one splurge a month

Instead of going out for an expensive dinner once a month, turn that dinner into a meal prepared at home. You'll save quite a bit even if you prepare something very fancy in your own kitchen.

Set up a carpool

Find someone that lives fairly close to you that works where you do and start carpooling together. Even if you can only do it a few days a week, you'll still drastically cut down on your commute costs, plus it will be a lot harder to stop for those impulse splurges.

Use public transportation
Even better, get in the habit of using public transportation for your commuting needs. Most metropolitan areas have surprisingly good public transportation options – and they're far cheaper (and not all that much more time consuming) than driving yourself.

Get on the bike
Want to start getting in better shape? Only live a mile or two from your work? That's a perfect situation to get a bike and start using it for the commute instead of wasting your dollars on gas and car maintenance.

Trim unnecessary monthly bills
Are you subscribing to Netflix but rarely using it? Cut it! Are you paying for premium cable channels that you never watch? Trim them!

Snowflake
Quite often, when people come into a bit of unexpected money, they tend to spend it without thinking about it. They decide not to stop for coffee, but then choose to spend it later on take out, for example. Instead of spending that "found money," take some or all of it and immediately put it into your emergency fund. If you have online banking, that's pretty easy – just transfer it out of your checking account.

*The key thing here is to **actually save this savings.** Instead of just spending the money on something else, put that money away towards your emergency fund. If you find that you're actually saving more than $50 a week with these tactics, then put more into the emergency fund or increase the amount you're putting into your retirement savings.*

Make It Automatic

So, you've trimmed $50 a week from your spending, but now you have this cash sitting there and it's tempting to spend it on something more exciting than an emergency fund. You're tempted...

... but you don't have to be tempted. Instead, you can set up an automatic savings plan to sweep that money straight out of your checking account and into your savings account that you're using for an emergency fund.

*If you haven't already, I recommend setting up **an online savings account at a bank separate than the one you normally do business with** for your emergency fund. Doing this not only lets you shop around for a bank with good service and good savings account rates, but it also causes you to put the money in a place that's not quite so easy to access. You can't just run to the ATM or stop by the teller window and withdraw cash from it – you have to go to your computer, order a transfer, and wait for a day or two to access the cash, which is more than enough time for you to think carefully about what you're doing and not get sucked in by impulse.*

*So, **sign up for an online savings account with good service and a solid interest rate, set up an automatic plan at that bank to sweep $50** (or whatever you can save) **a week into that savings account, and then forget about it.** Since you've already freed up that money through tightening your belt just a bit, this should be quite easy to do.*

Set Reasonable Milestones Along the Way
In a few months, you'll hit that first milestone – and it'll feel good. That account will have enough money in it that it'll start earning a bit of interest on its own and you'll start to feel in control of the situation.

Now's the time to keep going. Set another goal – an emergency fund of $1,000. Keep that automatic savings plan in place.

Once you reach that goal, aim for a single month's worth of living expenses. Then two months. Then three. And just keep watching that emergency fund grow.

Obviously, when you do have an emergency, tap that fund. Don't put your car repair bill on the credit card. Don't start living on plastic while you're between jobs. Instead, keep living a financially stable life thanks to your planning ahead.

You might just find that this is a lot of fun – so you might start seeking out more ways to save. Just keep setting goals for yourself and keep pushing yourself just a little to make it there.

Before you know it, your life won't be disrupted by these kinds of emergencies – and you'll sleep a lot better at night knowing that.[12]

---

[12] http://www.thesimpledollar.com/a-step-by-step-guide-to-building-a-big-healthy-emergency-fund/

Make more money

And now for the extra work. Here is a list of P/T ways to generate additional income to get that Emergency Fund started. Just a note, after funding your Emergency /Rainy Day Fund, you might want to consider continuing to work 'extra' to make your debt free journey move faster.

Online Side Hustling Ideas

For most people, an online side hustle is the easiest way to get started; you can find free WiFi a lot of places and the startup costs are minimal.

Sell on eBay – eBay is a great place to sell stuff and earn money, especially if you have something collectible. One of my favorite ways to side hustle on eBay is to go to estate sales and find items that you can purchase for cheap, then resell online. Just make sure that you keep the fees in consideration.

Sell on Amazon.com – Do you have old books, CDs, or DVDs? Then you should consider selling them on Amazon. It's incredibly easy to list your items to sell, and you'd be surprised how much you can get for old stuff sometimes. If you're a college student looking to sell your old textbooks, you should compare the Amazon prices to your bookstore buyback prices. Amazon is often a better place to sell.

Sell on Fiverr.com – Fiverr is a micro-selling site where you can sell all kinds of random projects, from design work to simply recording yourself on video talking about a brand.

Just Search the Internet – Do you search the Internet? Want to get paid for it? Swagbucks is a site that rewards you for doing various online tasks like taking surveys, watching videos, and using their search engine. When using their search engine, you get reward points after several searches, usually in the amount of 10-15 points. You can start cashing out rewards at the 500 points mark.

Fill Out Online Surveys – If you have some time to spare online, you could spend it filling out online surveys. There are sites that will pay you to do so and it's very easy. All you have to do is register, and these companies will contact you when they have a survey that fits your profile. Typically, these are online market research surveys for big brands.

Some of the most popular online survey sites include:

- ProOpinion – You can earn cash for filling out online surveys.
Nielson's National Consumer Panel – You can earn cash and gift cards for participating.
  - iPoll – Earn cash, gift cards, and more.
  - Harris Poll – This company is run by Neilson, and gives great rewards for filling out surveys.
  - Opinion Outpost – Earn cash for filling out surveys.
  - Survey Spot – Earn cash and rewards for filling out surveys and sharing your opinion.
  - Pinecone – You can earn $3 per survey you complete.

Online Coaching or Consulting – Beyond blogging, you can also become a coach or consultant for others, especially if you have some skills that people are looking for. Maybe you're a social media maven, or you have great online business skills. Selling your time and hopping on a Skype call or Google hangout is a great hustle.

Online Freelancing – There is a lot of freelance work online. You can sign up for sites like UpWork.

Sell Crafts on Etsy.com – Are you creative? Maybe selling your own creative products is the way to go. You could open a shop on Etsy and sell your crafts to others who are looking for unique products. You could sell paper goods like cards and invitations, or even home decor products themed around the holidays.

eBook Publishing – Have a story you want to tell? Maybe you should write an eBook and sell them on Amazon or Barnes and Noble.

Sell Stock Photos – Perhaps taking pictures is your forte. If you are a great photographer, you could possibly sell your photos online. Sites like iStockPhoto are always looking for contributors, who get paid a royalty every time their photo is purchased. This could be a great way to turn your art into some extra cash.

Blogging – Blogging is a great side hustle because you can do it at your own pace anywhere you want. It's not a quick and easy way to make money, but there are a lot of ways to make money side hustling while blogging. You can sell advertising, become an affiliate for other people's products, sell your own online product, and more.

Do Micro-Tasks on Mechanical Turk – Another micro-task site is Amazon's Mechanical Turk. The gigs on this site pay incredibly low amounts – less than a nickel typically. However, they take seconds, and you can earn around $6 per hour if you keep at it.

Do User Testing – Sites like UserTesting.com User are always looking for users to rate and give feedback about websites. Website owners post gigs to the site, and you simply login and give feedback and usability ratings on different websites and online apps.

Create A Course Online – Do you have something you can teach? You can teach something online at sites like Udemy.com. There are courses online for just about anything, and you can charge whatever pricing you feel is right for your instruction.

Become a Virtual Assistant – Do you enjoy writing, social media, and blogging, but don't want to start your own blog? You can find virtual assistant jobs where you help other people run their sites and social media accounts.

Sometimes, working offline when you side hustle is a more lucrative prospect – especially depending on your skill set.

Tutor – Are you a college student who has already taken several classes in your major? You could help tutor others in those same classes and earn upwards of $20-$50 per session. It's a great way to side hustle in school, while keeping your own knowledge sharp.

Be A Task Rabbit – TaskRabbit.com is a place where you can sign up and run small tasks for others. It can include anything from picking up the groceries to cleaning or helping people move. Typical tasks take a few hours, but there are a lot of tasks available in most large cities.

Catering – Do you want to side hustle just on Friday and Saturday nights? Well, you should team up with a catering company, as they often need servers and wait staff just for the events they host on the weekend. Many companies are "call-in", which means you can work when you choose to.

Cleaning Service – If you like to clean, you could help clean houses. These can be ongoing side hustles, like a weekly or bi-weekly service, or one time deals (such as for when people move). You could even join forces with some friends and tackle larger projects.

Baby-Sitting – Baby-sitting is another great side hustle that can earn you upwards of $100 per night! Many people start baby sitting in high school, but there's no reason that college students and other young adults can't keep in the game, especially if you have neighbors or relatives with young children.

Computer Repair – Are you tech savvy? Maybe you can help your friends and neighbors with computer repair, from updating and installing the latest operating system to helping them get a virus off their computer. If you have the know-how, people will pay.

Recycle – Recycling can be a great way to earn some extra money. I'm not talking about becoming a bum at the park rummaging for cans (although you can do that) – I'm talking about encouraging your friends and neighbors to leave their cans and bottles aside for you. If you want to take it up a notch, look for recycling metal and scrap to get even more money.

Resume Help – Are you working at a company right now and see a lot of resumes? Do you hire people? Perhaps you can help others with their resumes and cover letters (for a fee, of course).

Dog Walking – Do you have friends or neighbors with dogs? Do they work in the day? Maybe you can offer your services to them as a dog walker. Not only is this a great side hustle that can earn you a little extra cash, but it also gets you exercising every day.

Estate Sales – Instead of just selling stuff on eBay, you can also host estate sales. To be successful, though, you're going to need to get some friends involved to help.

Handyman Work – Do you have a knack for home repair? Then you could side hustle as a handyman on nights and weekends to earn a little bit of extra money. Just be up front about your skills set – repairing fences, doing small plumbing jobs, whatever it happens to be.

Housesitting – One of the easiest side hustles to do: simply sit and sleep in someone's house while they are out of town. This is a great side hustle, but too bad it's usually not a consistent revenue stream for most.

Hauling Service – Do you have a truck? You could sell your services helping other people haul stuff to the dump, or even picking up large items at places like Home

Depot. Don't have a truck? You could work at a hauling company and do the manual labor for others.

Modeling – This is the side hustle for the good-looking people of the world. You can go to school or work, and still take modeling jobs at night and on the weekends. For many models, there isn't always a steady stream of work, but if you have success at a few gigs, this could become very lucrative.

Movie or TV Extra – Depending on where you live, you could become an extra on a TV show or movie. Many studios are always looking for a steady stream of extras, and you can get paid a couple hundred dollars for just standing or walking around in the back of a movie set.

Mystery Shopping – Do you enjoy fast food or going into retail shops? Many companies hire mystery shoppers to test the customer service of their stores. A common one is Subway, which hires mystery shoppers to ensure that "Sandwich Artists" are following all the franchise guidelines. If you have time and can travel to different places, this could be a good side hustle.

Pet Sitting – If you love pets, taking care of your friends' and neighbors' pets while they are out of town can be a great way to earn some extra cash. It can be fun to make a new furry friend and get paid for it at the same time.

Join A Research Study or Focus Group – Have you walked through a college campus and seen the flyer for research studies and focus groups? Companies are always looking for people's opinions about products and services, and for sitting in one of these groups for a few hours, you could earn upwards of $100.

Moving Service – If you have time on the weekends, and are okay lifting heavy boxes and furniture, you could join up with a moving service and get paid to help people move. It's not easy work, but most people tip the movers as well.

Gardening Service – A lot of entrepreneurs got their start mowing lawns, and it's still a great side hustle today. If you live in an area where people need gardeners, knock on doors and offer your gardening services. It's a great way to earn some extra cash.

Painting Service – Painting services are another common side hustle for college students. If you have time on weekends and during the summer, you can paint houses or join a painting company. It's not easy, but it can pay well in the right neighborhoods.

Pool Cleaning Service – Pool cleaning is another one that can be easy money, as long as you know how to do it. Matt Giovanisci started cleaning pools, and then turned it into a great side hustle at SwimUniversity.com

Become Someone's Friend – Join a service like Rentafriend.com, where you can get paid to become someone's friend for a period of time. This is strictly platonic stuff here.

Shoveling Snow – In the winter in many parts of the country, this can be a lucrative side hustle.

Micro-Entrepreneurship Ideas

These ideas are a little different than the typical hustle – they are more based on entrepreneurship and asset leveraging to make even more money for you. These can lead to passive income over time if done well.

Rent Your House on AirBNB – If you travel a lot, you have the potential to rent out your house while you're away on vacation.

Become an Uber or Lyft Driver – Another set-your-own-schedule business is driving people around. All you need is a car and some spare time. Just sign up with Uber or Lyft and start driving people around. You'll make what you put into it.

Become a PostMate – Similar to Uber or Lyft, except you're delivering food instead of people. PostMates is an on-demand delivery service where you get paid around $20 per hour to deliver food. In fact, right now you are guaranteed to earn $1,000 per 60 deliveries in New York or San Francisco. That's not bad.

Agent Anything – Agent Anything is outsourcing geared to students. People post projects on the site and you can make offers for how much you're willing to pay to help. Most gigs on the site earn anywhere from $20 to $100, but some earn more..

Renting Out A Room – If you have a spare room in your house, you could make some extra money by renting it out. You have to advertise, screen tenants, and collect rent, but the small amount of time involved could be lucrative.

Renting Out Your Garage or Driveway – If you have extra space in your driveway (or side yard), you could rent that space out as well to people looking to store property, like boats or RVs. In many areas, there are HOAs that prevent people from parking this type of equipment, and you could help solve that problem for them while earning a little extra cash.

Impel At Work

Sometimes, side hustling isn't about starting something else, but it's really about making better use of the job you currently have.

Volunteer for Overtime – If you are working at a job, this might not be a true side hustle, but it is a way to earn some extra money fast. In many companies, you can volunteer to work longer and earn extra pay. If you don't have an idea on what side hustle to do right now, this could be an option.

Employee Referral Program – Again, not a true side hustle, but a great way to earn extra money. Many companies offer referral programs where you can earn anywhere from $25 to $1,000 per employee you refer. That could go a long way.

Tuition Reimbursement Program – Many companies also offer tuition reimbursement programs to help pay for school. Maybe your short term hustle is to better your education. Why not have your company pay for it while you're at it?

Get A Part Time Job – Finally, if you don't want to work for yourself, go spend your time hustling for someone else at a part time job. While not ideal for some, it can be a great way to earn some extra money in your spare time[13]

---

[13] http://thecollegeinvestor.com/14608/make-money-fast-side-hustling/

Weekly Spending Tracker/ Where is your money going?

Now that you have some ideas to fund your emergency fund, it's time to start tracking where are you are currently spending money? Use the following charts to list **ALL** of the purchases that you make over the next 7 days. From that chocolate candy bar to filing up your gas tank.

Daily Spending Chart – Monday

Amount Spent	Item

Daily Spending Chart – Tuesday

Amount Spent	Item

Daily Spending Chart – Wednesday

Amount Spent	Items Purchased

Daily Spending Chart – Thursday

Amount Spent	Items Purchased

Daily Spending Chart – Friday

Amount Spent	Items Purchased

Daily Spending Chart – Saturday

Amount Spent	Items Purchased

Daily Spending Chart – Sunday

Amount Spent	Item Purchased

Take some time to study the past weeks spending. Is there a theme? Do you see a pattern of where your money has been slipping away? If so, list some potential changes that you can make to cut down on the unnecessary spending.

_____
_____
_____
_____
_____
_____
_____
_____
_____
_____

Calculating Your Total Debt

This chapter will probably be your *Come to Jesus moment*. You will need to be completely **HONEST** with yourself. Below, it is necessary to list **ALL** of your Debts. As small as the $20 that you owe your grandmother to the amounts owed on your vehicle and home. Breath deeply – and then start writing.

List of Debts As Of: _____

Whom Debt Is Owed	Amount Owed	Whom Debt Is Owed	Amount Owed

Total Amount of Debts :_____

REST HERE.

FOR A MINUTE.

ITS OKAY.

The above number will probably cause some type of emotion. You might be shocked.
You might chuckle. You might think it's wrong and add the figures again. I cried and
then wondered how did I allow myself to create so much debt, and then I remembered,
so I stopped crying.

Regardless to your response, the process of filling out the chart was critical. Now you
have a much clearer idea of the challenge that you are facing and you can move on
to the next step now.

Calculating Your Income

Now that all your debts have been listed, it is time to list all your incoming income. Fill in the charts below. If you are paid twice a month, only fill in the first two charts. In the last chart, combine the numbers to calculate your total monthly income.

Week 1 Income

Income (After Tax)	Amount
Income #1	
Income #2	
Other	
Total Income	

Week 2 Income

Income (After Tax)	Amount
Income #1	
Income #2	
Other	
Total Income	

Week 3 Income

Income (After Tax)	Amount
Income #1	
Income #2	
Other	
Total Income	

Week 4 Income

Income (After Tax)	Amount
Income #1	
Income #2	
Other	
Total Income	

Total Monthly Income

Income (After Tax)	Amount
Income #1	
Income #2	
Other	
Total Income	

Fixed Expenses

The next chart that needs to be reviewed is the list of your Fixed Expenses.

A fixed expenses is "any expense that does not change from period to period," such as mortgage or rent payments, utility bills, and loan payments. The amounts may vary slightly, which may be the case with utilities, but you know they are due on a regular basis. Here is a list of categories to include in your fixed expenses:

Mortgage(s)
Rent
Property taxes (if paying monthly)
Strata fee / condo fee
House / tenant insurance
Utility bills (cable, cell, electricity, water, etc.)
Lease / car loan payment
Vehicle insurance (if paying monthly)
Life / Disability / Extended health (or other) insurance
Bank fees[14]

Fixed Expenses	Amount
Charity	
Savings	

[14] http://www.mymoneycoach.ca/blog/what-are-fixed-savings-variable-costs-expenses-and-learn-to-budget-money.html

Housing – Mortgage/Rent	
Electric	
Gas	
Water	
Phone	
Cable	
Sewer/Trash	
Internet	
Food	
Credit Card #1	
Credit Card #2	
Credit Card #3	
Credit Card #4	
Loan Payment	
Car Payment #1	
Car Payment #2	

Auto Repair and Tags	
Auto Gas	
Auto Insurance	
General Merchandise	
Clothes	
Haircuts	
Gifts – Birthdays/Holidays	
Social and Entertainment	
Other	
Other	
Other	
Other	
Other	
Total Expenses	
Surplus / Shortage	

Irregular Expenses

Also important are the list of your irregular expenses. You might need to give this a little extra thought.

Irregular expenses are costs that come up throughout the year, that you need to budget your money properly for or else you'll find yourself reaching for a credit card when those expenses comes up. You must save for these expenses in advance, and not feel guilty when you spend the money. Consider it "planned spending." Examples of irregular expenses include:

Property taxes (if paying quarterly or annually)
House insurance (if paying annually)
Vehicle insurance (if paying quarterly or annually)
Clothing & shoes (if you shop once or twice per year)
Health expenses
Vet bills
Gifts
Vehicle maintenance[15]

---

[15] http://www.mymoneycoach.ca/blog/what-are-fixed-savings-variable-costs-expenses-and-learn-to-budget-money.html

Irregular Expenses	Amount
Property Taxes	
Home Owners Insurance	
Car Insurance	
Clothing and Shoes	
Health Expenses	
Gifts	
Car Maintenance	
Other	
Other	
Other	
Other	

Variable Costs

The definition of variable costs can differ, but we like to define them as anything you can buy in a store (for example groceries, gas, or coffee) or expenses that are within your control. You can decide how much and if you will spend on these items. Here is a list of what you can include in your variable expenses category:

Groceries
Personal care items (drugstore)
Fuel / public transportation costs
Parking
Clothing & shoes
Daycare
Work lunches & snacks
Eating out
Entertainment
Tobacco / alcohol
Lottery
Babysitting
Sports & recreation, other hobbies
Hair care / salon services
Magazines / newspapers / books
Children's lessons and activities[16]

---

[16] http://www.mymoneycoach.ca/blog/what-are-fixed-savings-variable-costs-expenses-and-learn-to-budget-money.html

Irregular Expenses	Amount
(List Your Irregular Expenses Below)	

Using all the previous Expenses Charts, what are your total monthly expenses:

$_____

*You can factor in your irregular expenses by adding the total amount of the cost during the year and then dividing that number by 12. The will give the monthly cost.

****

This above amount is the bare minimum that your income must be. And please note, when I say minimum, that means poverty and living paycheck to paycheck, with no means to handle any type of Emergency that you might encounter.

Now, to pay down debt and create a financial buffer zone, your total income must be higher than your listed expenses. The larger the difference, the faster you can become debt free.

Go back to the Income Chart and write down your total amount of monthly income:

$_____

Use the space below to express you financial thoughts after completing the charts exercise.

_____
_____
_____
_____
_____
_____
_____
_____

The B Word (Budget)

Unlike most people, you know how much money you have coming in and you also know where your money is going out. Guess what, it's time to create a budget.

Organizing Your Money (Telling your money where to go)

Zero Based Budgets

Zero-based budgeting is an approach to planning and decision-making that reverses the working process of traditional budgeting. In traditional incremental budgeting, departmental managers justify only variances versus past years based on the assumption that the "baseline" is automatically approved.

	A	Jan 6, 2012	Jan 13, 2012	Jan 20, 2012	Jan 27, 2012
1		Jan 6, 2012	Jan 13, 2012	Jan 20, 2012	Jan 27, 2012
2	Giving	$100.00	$100.00	$100.00	$100.00
3	Mortgage	$400.00	$400.00	$400.00	$400.00
4	Car Payment	$150.00	$150.00	$0.00	$0.00
5	Water & Sewer	$0.00	$0.00	$35.00	$35.00
6	Cable	$50.00	$0.00	$50.00	$0.00
7	Telephone		$50.00	$0.00	$50.00
8	Savings	$100.00	$100.00	$100.00	$100.00
9	Groceries	$100.00	$100.00	$100.00	$100.00
10	Credit Card	$100.00	$0.00	$0.00	$0.00
11	Clothing			$200.00	
12					
13	Total Expenses	$1,000.00	$900.00	$985.00	$785.00
14					
15	Total Income	$1,000.00	$1,000.00	$1,000.00	$1,000.00
16	Total Unassigned	$0.00	$100.00	$15.00	$215.00

The fancy definition simple means give all of dollars a place to go – or all of your dollars will all go away. (smile) At first I had about 25 envelopes. I now have 3 envelopes – Gas, Entertainment, Groceries. I have gotten the other previous envelopes under control, meaning, I know how NOT to go over the budget.

Your Practice Zero-Based Budget (Weekly)

Practice telling your money where to go. List the amount of money that you weekly apply to each of these categories:

	Week 1	Week 2	Week 3	Week 4
Giving/Charity				
Rent/Mortgage				
Electric				
Heat				
Groceries				
Car Note				
Internet				
Phone				
Restaurants				
Gas				
Entertainment				
Clothing				
Travel				
Other				
Total Expenses				
(Your) Total Income				
Total $$ Unassigned (or amount short)				

Here is another example of a Zero-Based budget

This family has a budget of $2,500. During the month of April, they were over budget. They were under budget during May. This simply means that they would have more money to be applied towards their Snowball Debt Elimination.

This family budgeted $90.00 for Heat, however they spend $100.00. They also under-budgeted Restaurants ($42.00) Gas ($15.00) and clothing ($65.00) for a total of $89.00.

However, in the month of May, with the exception of Groceries (-20.00) all of the categories were on point, which left them with an extra $135 for that month.

	April			May		
	Budget	Actual	Variance	Budget	Actual	Variance
Income	2,500	2,500	0	2,500	2,500	0
Expenses						
Rent	800	800	0	800	800	0
Electric	50	50	0	50	45	5
Heat	90	100	(10)	90	80	10
Internet	50	50	0	50	50	0
Phone	50	50	0	50	50	0
Groceries	200	189	11	200	220	(20)
Restaurants	150	192	(42)	150	100	50
Gas	100	115	(15)	100	100	0
Entertainment	100	95	5	100	100	0
Clothing	60	125	(65)	60	40	20
Travel	50	25	25	50	50	0
Other	100	98	2	100	30	70
Total Expenses	1,800	1,889	(89)	1,800	1,665	135
Balance	700	611	89	1,400	835	(135)

Your Practice Zero-Based Budget (Monthly)

It's your turn. Take a week and tell you dollars where to go. Keep all of your receipts and at the end of the week and check to see if your money went where you told it to go.

	Budget	Actual	Variance
Income			
Expenses			
Giving/Charity			
Rent/Mortgage			
Electric			
Heat			
Groceries			
Car Note			
Internet			
Phone			
Restaurants			
Gas			
Entertainment			
Clothing			
Travel			
Other			
Total Expenses			
Balance			

Using Envelopes With Your Zero-Based Budget

A Way To Control Spending: The Envelope System

The Envelope System – Getting Started With A Budget

The first thing you have to do when you're trying to control your spending is to set up a budget. If you don't know where the money is going and what your set expenses are, it will be difficult to setup a working budget or envelope system.

Tracking our expenses was relatively easy because we log pretty much every dollar coming in or out in Microsoft Money. We have a good 1-2 years of history right at our fingertips. With that we were able to see exactly how much we were spending on set expenses (mortgage, utilities, taxes), as well as other categories where the spending was out of control (food, shopping).

Once you've got a good baseline for what you need to spend every month on the basics, you'll want to set up a monthly cash flow plan, and give every dollar a name through doing a zero based budget. What that means is every single dollar of income that comes into the household will be allocated, and assigned a job. If you make $5000 of net income, all $5000 of that should be allocated either to an expense or savings category. That way you won't have the extra money (after expenses) disappearing into the ether. It gets saved, or assigned to a debt, or gets some other job. Your money works for you instead of just melting away.

So to review, the first steps you'll want to take include*:*

1. out your regular monthly set expenses.
*2. **Figure out other variable expenses** (like food, shopping, entertainment) and assign a realistic dollar amount for that category in the budget.*
*3. **Put together a zero-based budget** where every dollar of income and expense is allocated. Every dollar has a name and a job.*

Setting Up Your Envelope System

Once you've got a budget setup, and you know how much you want to spend on each category, it's time to setup your envelope system. The idea behind the envelopes is that it helps you control your spending on certain problem categories by giving you a set amount of money each month in your envelope that you need to use towards that category. When the money is gone from the envelope, you can't spend any more money on that category. If you absolutely need to spend more, you have to take money from another category to fill in the gaps.

We have a couple of big problem categories that we consistently overspend in. Eating out/restaurant spending and shopping spending. My wife and I love eating out, and in some ways eating out has become our way to connect with each other and entertain ourselves. If we have a date night we go out to a nice restaurant and enjoy an evening together. The problem is that we're doing it way too often, and spending way too much money doing it. The solution? We added these problem categories to our envelope system. In the picture below you can see our envelope for "restaurants".

We also set up envelopes for some other categories with variable expenses including groceries, shopping, entertainment and "blow money" (personal money we can spend for every and any reason). Whenever we get paid we are now going to withdraw money for each spending category and place that money in the envelope.

For example, if in our budget we allocate $400/month for groceries, we'll withdraw $200 from the first of the month's paychecks and put $200 in the envelope. Whenever we go shopping for food we can then only spend money from that "groceries" envelope, up until the point the money is gone. If we go shopping and the bill comes up to $201, we must take that $1 from another envelope, or put back $1 worth of food. For the last paycheck of the month, we'll once again withdraw $200 for food and add it to the envelope. If we've only spent $100 the first two weeks we'll then have $300 in the envelope. At the end of the month, if you have money left over, decide how to allocate that money – either putting it towards debt, or saving it.

Using this system may be a bit uncomfortable at first, especially if you're using envelopes for a larger number of categories. We know of one couple who set up a ton of spending categories using this system, and then ended up withdrawing thousands every month and putting it into envelopes. We decided it would be easier to just choose some of our biggest overspending *categories and withdraw the money for those. It comes out to about $800/month that we're withdrawing and putting in envelopes.*

So the envelope system boils down to this*:*
Set up a zero-based budget, and know how much you should spend in all categories.
Find some of your biggest over-spending categories, or places where the expenses vary quite a bit every month and set up an envelope for those categories.

Every paycheck withdraw enough cash to fully fund the envelopes for your envelope system.

Only spend what you have in the envelopes, and if you don't have any money left , don't spend. If you need to spend more, take it from another envelope.
Any money that is left over, either save or put towards your debt snowball (if you have debts).

While we're still setting up our envelopes, we know from watching others use the system that it can have a dramatic effect on how much money you're spending. Not only are you setting limits on yourself and actually living on a budget, you're spending cash, which hurts more.

Studies have shown that when you use a credit card, even if you're paying it off every month, you spend on average 12-18% more. Using cash for those problem categories will help you to rein in that spending, and force you to not spend more than you make.[17]

---

[17] http://www.biblemoneymatters.com/a-way-to-control-spending-the-envelope-system/

Getting Ready to Create Your Budget

The **Debt Snowball** and the **Debt Avalanche** are the two main strategies for paying down your debt. The **Debt Snowball** method says you should start by paying off the credit cards or loans with the lowest balances first, while the **Debt Avalanche** method tells you to pay off the accounts with the highest interest rates first.

Which plan is right for you?

From a strictly financial standpoint, the debt avalanche technique is always going to cost you less than the debt snowball would. Nevertheless, the time and money you stand to save by using the avalanche does you absolutely no good if you can't maintain the motivation to follow it through to the end.

Take a hard look at your personal financial situation and be very upfront with yourself. If you find it easy to defer instant gratification in favor of future benefits, then debt avalanche is probably going to be the repayment plan for you.
But if you find it difficult to stay focused on long-term goals, and especially if you've had a hard time paying down large balances in the past, debt snowball can be a great way to build responsible repayment habits through small, manageable steps.[18]

---

[18] https://www.creditkarma.com/article/how-to-pay-off-your-debt

Debt Snowball

The Debt Snowball method involves paying off your smallest balances first to create momentum and encourage you to keep slaying those debts. This strategy empowers you to stay on track by helping you view your debt as more manageable and less intimidating every step of the way:

- *At the onset, you're going to be paying off cards as quickly as possible, since you're focusing all of your extra money on the smallest balance you owe.* If you're paying on five accounts every month, but can completely pay off two of them within a year, you can cut the number of bills you have to keep track of almost in half! Juggling fewer payments can reduce stress and your larger balances will be easier to cope with when they're the only bills you have to worry about.
- *Each time you pay off a debt, you have one less minimum payment to make.* As you whittle away at your smaller debts, you can take the money that was going toward your minimum payments and fold it in to make larger payments on your larger balances. If you have five debts and each one has a $25 minimum payment, by the time you're tackling your largest debt, you'll have an extra $100 to put towards it every month.

The debt snowball plan helps you build confidence and positive repayment habits by prioritizing the "easy" debts first. Having a few victories under your belt could be just what you need to pump yourself up to tackle your largest debts.

Retail card	$100	**+$100**							
Credit card 2	$120	Credit card 2	$220	**+$220**					
Credit card 1	$135	Credit card 1	$135	Credit card 1	$355	**+$355**			
Car loan	$255	Car loan	$255	Car loan	$255	Car loan	$610	**+$610**	
Mortgage	$870	Mortgage	$870	Mortgage	$870	Mortgage	$870	Mortgage	$1,480
Total	**$1,480**	**Total**	**$1,480**	**Total**	**$1,480**	**Total**	**$1,480**	**Total**	**$1,480**

List your personal notes below:

_____

_____

_____

_____

_____

_____

_____

_____

Practice Chart – List 5 of your Debts and using the Debt Snowball System practice paying them down.

Bill #1 $Amount	After Bill #1 is Paid			
Bill #2 $Amount		After Bill #2 is Paid		
Bill #3 $Amount			After Bill #3 is Paid	
Bill #4 $Amount				After Bill #4 is Paid
Bill #5 $Amount				

Debt Avalanche

The Debt Avalanche method involves paying off your balances with the highest interest rates first. This plan prioritizes efficiency and aims to be the indisputably cheapest and fastest way to get out of debt.

- **Paying your highest interest balances first saves you money.** There's no getting around the fact that high interest costs you, especially when you carry a balance long enough for your interest to compound. When this happens, the interest you've already been charged gets added to your principal balance, so you'll be charged interest on it.
- **Paying your highest interest balances first saves you time.** The longer it's going to take you to pay off your debt, the more you will benefit from the avalanche. When you don't pay off your high interest debts first, they will continue to accrue and compound interest, increasing faster than your lower interest debts would in the same amount of time. Depending on the details of your personal financial situation, not only can the snowball cost you thousands in interest, it can also cost you months of repayment.

If saving money is the only motivation you need, think about trying out this strategy.[19]

---

[19] https://www.creditkarma.com/article/how-to-pay-off-your-debt

Name of Issuing Bank	Balance	APR (interest rate)
Citibank: Cash Advance	500	29%
Target (TD Bank)	2,000	25%
Citibank: Purchase	3,000	19%
Chase	3,000	15%
Chase	2,000	0%
Total	**10,000**	*16.65%*

List your personal notes below:

_____
_____
_____
_____
_____
_____
_____
_____

Paying Bills – Your Organization Calendar

The first thing that I must mention is, getting out of debt takes **EXTREME** detail and the ability to be Pro-Active not Re-Active. This might be a new concept for some of us, however, it is important to Pay our bill **BEFORE** it is due… not on the due date. This takes planning, practice and organization. It might also take a few months of sticking to your budget to do able to do.

Calendar

First, I purchased an oversized desk calendar and a package of highlighter markers. To start organizing, gather all of your bills. And list the due dates of each bill on the calendar, alone with the amount due. Having a calendar that is color coordinated will make it easier to read at a glance. So in addition to purchasing a large desk top calendar, you will also need to purchase a package of highlighter markers.

The important dates to highlight are Paydays, Bills Due Dates, Planned Entertainment Days. Each of these categories will have their own individual color. As an example:

1 – Paydays = Green Highlight
2 – Bill Due Dates = Pink Highlight
3 – Planned Entertainment Days = Blue Highlight
4 – ***Anything else that is money related*** = Color of your choice

When the bill is paid, I draw a large 'x' over the date, thus indicating that it has been paid. Just a note, in the section called, "Stop living paycheck to paycheck", you will learn how to get ahead on your fixed expenses.

Who gets paid first?

If you are behind in all or most of your bills, it is imperative that you follow the plan of what Debt Guru Dave Ramsey refers to as the 4 walls.

The 4 Walls

1. Food

Feed your family.

Set aside a sufficient amount of money in the budget for food. This should include "eating out" money. I also recommend adding everything to the grocery budget that you would buy at the supermarket — maybe call it your Walmart Fund or Target Fund, depending on your preference.

It's always better to overbudget in the food category. Be reasonable when determining the amount of money your household will spend on food and groceries. After budgeting for a few months, you will have a better understanding of how much your family actually needs for food. If your kids are fed, that's one less thing to worry about.

2. Shelter

Pay your house payment or rent and keep the lights on.

The shelter budget category should include everything needed to keep you and your family safe and warm inside your home — mortgage or rent, utilities, etc.

Never pay a credit card bill instead of your house payment. You can afford to have a little ding on your credit. You cannot afford to lose your house or have the heat or power disconnected. As Dave Ramsey says, "if you have to choose to be behind on something ... choose to be behind on things that don't matter as much."

Keeping the lights on and paying your house payment should give you one less thing to worry about.

So far, the family is fed and the lights are on. This is good.

3. Transportation

You need to keep the car moving so you can get to work and make some money.

Car payments, gasoline expenses, car insurance and basic repairs and maintenance needed to keep the car running fall under this category.

When budgeting for fuel expenses, again be reasonable. It's better to overbudget for fuel than underbudget and not be able to fill your tank with gas. After you do the budget for several months, this category will become easier to project.

Also, do some simple math to determine how much money you will need to set aside each month to cover the regular maintenance on your vehicles. That way when the car needs an oil change or new tires, you will have the money to cover it. You have to keep the car running.

Don't pay another debt instead of paying your car loan. You cannot afford to have your car repossessed.

Food is on the table, a roof is over your head and gasoline is in the car. You're OK.

4. Clothing

This category works a little differently. A large clothing budget is probably not a priority for everyone. If you're just a single guy or girl and you don't have a bunch of money, you probably don't need a bunch of new clothes. But if you have a family and kids, you need a clothing budget.

If you have young children, then you know they grow out of their clothes weekly. Or if you have kids in school then they will probably need new clothes and new shoes before school starts. Plan for this in your budget.

Project how much money you think your family will need for new clothes for the entire year, divide that number by 12 and set aside that amount of money each month for clothing. That way you will have the money needed when the kids grow overnight or when school unexpectedly starts tomorrow.

Be frugal with your clothing purchases if your budget is tight — or just be frugal always. There are a lot of ways to save money when buying clothes and shoes. Don't be afraid to hit up the thrift stores, garage sales or get hand-me-downs from your relatives, friends and neighbors. Hey, my mom made my shorts when I was a kid. I survived.

Kids are always outgrowing their clothes. Somebody somewhere is throwing out some good stuff.

The family is fed, the lights are on, gasoline is in the car and the kids aren't naked. You've covered the four walls.

Taking care of these things first will help simplify the budget and ease the stress and worry of your household finances. The rest is basically a game. If you can't pay your credit card bill or the annoying bill collector that calls and harasses you daily, don't sweat it. You will get to it. Take care of your own first. Secure your household and family before anything else and then take care of the other things.
Family first. [20]

Binders

The secondary phase of organizing includes the creation of a Home Management Binder System. This will consist of 3 separate binders.

1 – Monthly Bills
2 – Snowball Debt or Avalanche Debt
3 – Home Management

Additionally, you will need to purchase paper protectors and a package of binder dividers.

After listing all of you bill information on the calendar, place the actual bill into a paper protector. This will include all of your fixed expenses and maybe a few of your irregular expenses too. Make it a point to request the paper version of all of your bills, do not go Paperless! Each of your bills will have their own individual paper protector. Each month use a new protector and place the bill in front of the previous month's bill. When the bill is paid, write a note on the bill - the day that it was paid as well as a reference number if one is available.

The second binder, as I mentioned is the Snowball Debt Eliminator or Avalanche Binder. Again, have paper protectors for each and every debt that is included. Make sure that you document ALL communications with ANYONE that you speak with regarding the bill that you are calling about. (Or the debt collector that called you), In

---

[20] http://www.deseretnews.com/article/865602271/What-should-take-priority-in-your-monthly-budgets.html

addition to creating a large 'x' on your calendar, also document in writing, on the bill, the date that a payment was made along with the amount that was paid.

I have found that the best part of this binder, is when the debt is paid off, writing in big bold letters **PAID** along with drawing a **HUGE** smiley face. When the bill is paid off, placed the binder in the back of the pile. Leaving the next bill to be tackled as the new one in the front. When you need a charge of motivation, refer to the back of the binder and look at the smile faces. (**You Can Do It**)

The last binder is my Home Management Binder. This binder is constantly changing to serve the needs of whatever is important during that month or season.   A few potential forms that you might want to include you your binder are:

- Weekly Planner
- Family Mission Statement
- Emergency Preparedness
- Emergency & Child ID Information
- Grocery Shopping, Recipes, Weekly Menu
- Home Maintenance Sections
- Crafts
- House Rules
- Project Planner
- Kids Guide to Chores
- Family Tree
- Financial Forms and Budget/Debt Information

Note – All of these types of forms are downloadable online. Additionally, each year I change the color of my binders.

Creating a household notebook for the first time is a concrete manifestation of your desire to improve things in your home.

Creating a homemaking notebook also causes you to sit down and plan and set goals for your family and home.

Getting everything gathered together in your homemaking notebook helps you think about how all parts of your home and family members' lives fit together, like so many pieces of a puzzle, and to make sure you pay attention to all the puzzle pieces adequately.

Once you create your household management notebook you do not have to waste time trying to decide what to do first, or next. Instead, you have a plan, and you can work your plan.

Being able to put your finger on any piece of information needed, either in an emergency or in an everyday moment makes your life, and the lives of your family, so much more peaceful.

Sharing your household management binder with all the members of your family allows everyone to get involved as a team in taking care of your home and each other.

Most importantly, creating and using a household notebook helps you enjoy your home and family – the ultimate goal of household management. [21]

---

[21] http://www.household-management-101.com/home-management-binder.html

Creating A Bill Payment Schedule

Many people pay bills on the day that they are due, however, if you use your calendar and combined with your paydays, organization can be created. This example Monthly Bill Chart shows how you can create a schedule. Notice how all the fixed bills have been listed followed by listing the due dates of the bills. You can see in advance which bills can be paid using each of your paychecks. The paydays that are being used for this schedule are 12/23/16 – 1/6/17 – 1/20/17

Month __JANUARY_____ 201__7_____

What	How Much	Due	Paycheck Date	Paid
Mortgage	$660.00	1/1/17	12/23/16	12/25/16
Wifi	$50.00	1/2/17	12/23/16	12/25/16
Gas	$40.00	1/19/17	1/6/17	1/6/17
Electricity	$70.00	1/25/17	1/20/17	Automatic Transfer
Snowball	$160.00	1/22/17	1/20/17	Automatic Transfer

PayCheck 1	Paycheck 2
Charity - $40.00	Mortgage - $660.00
Wifi - $60.00	Travel - $150.00
Roku - $22.00	Electricity - $70.00
Cell - $80.00	Charity - $40.00
Fun Money - $50.00	Snowball - $160.00
Fun Money - $50.00	
Gas - $34.00	
Gasoline - $120.00	

List your personal thoughts:

_____
_____
_____
_____
_____
_____
_____

Ok, now it's your turn. List your monthly bills and then follow up with how they can be broken down and paid using your 2 or 3 paychecks for the following month.

Your Monthly Bill Chart

Month _____ 201_____

What(Bill)	How Much	Due	Paycheck Date	Paid

Using the due date of the bill, list them under Paycheck 1 or Paycheck 2. If you continue to follow this plan, in time you will be able to pay all your bills BEFORE the due date.

PayCheck 1	Paycheck 2

Just a note. Some bills can be broken into two paycheck payments. This is discussed further in the section: Getting 13 Mortgage Payments.

Tackling Big Bills Payment Plans and Settling Accounts

This is a very proactive activity and it has been my experience that the older the debt is, the more willing creditors are to work with you in terms of creating acceptable plans to pay it off.

I normally call my creditors once a month to attempt to establish payment plans that will fit into my budget. With each conversation, I take control. For example, if I had $100.00 a month to start paying a new debt, the conversation would be very specific that there is $100.00 in my budget and not a penny more. With one creditor, they informed me that would need a minimum of $125 per month to establish a payment plan. I simply informed them that their amount does not work with my budget and that now I would have to place them back at the bottom of my payment list. I added that I would call them again next month and please NOT to call me.

I would now move down the list to my next creditor to see if they could work with the $100.00 payment, always "ending with a "Thank you" and "Have a good day." End Call ~ No debates ~ No pleading ~ Just actual facts – this is what I have – do you want to make a deal? And if you do make a deal, make sure that you have your settlement agreement in writing!!!

Lastly, always make a note of the day of your call and whom you spoke with. Remember your organizational calendars and binders to keep you on track with your communications with creditors.

Settlements

Here's how to approach negotiation on debt settlement with a debt collector:

- **Determine what you can afford to pay.** *Review your budget. Do not offer more than you can afford. When you know how much you can afford, begin your negotiations by offering less.*

  When you negotiate with a debt collector do not provide bank account numbers, your place of employment, or references.

- **Ask the debt collector to remove all negative information from your credit records related to the settled debt that has been added to your records since the debt was turned over to him.** *(The debt collector cannot remove any negative information about your debt that was added to your credit files when the debt was still with the creditor.) Then check your credit histories to make sure that the negative information has been removed.*

- **Put the deal in writing.** *Get the details of the agreement in writing before you give the collector any money. It's also a good idea to hire a consumer law attorney to review the agreement. At a minimum, your agreement should clearly state:*
  - ○ **How much you have agreed to pay.**
  - ○ **Whether you will pay the settlement amount in a lump sum or over time.**
  - ○ **When the lump sum or payments are due.**
  - ○ **How you will make the payment(s), such as via an electronic bank transfer or with a cashier's check. Avoid giving a debt collector a personal check.**
  - ○ **That the debt collector agrees to report to the credit bureaus that your debt has been "paid in full" as soon as the settlement amount is received.**
  - ○ **Any concessions that the debt collector has agreed to make.**
  - ○ **Conditions that breach the agreement and the consequences of the breach.**
  - ○ **Do not sign the agreement until it reflects everything you agreed to and unless you understand everything in it.** *After you sign the agreement, make a copy for yourself and file it in a safe place.*

    If the debt collector won't put your agreement in writing, prepare an agreement yourself; sign it; and send it to the debt collector via certified mail, return receipt requested.

- *When you encounter a debt collector who refuses to negotiate, contact the creditor who turned your debt over to the debt collector. Find out if the creditor may be willing to work out an agreeable compromise.*

If you don't feel confident negotiating a debt settlement agreement, hire a consumer law attorney to do it for you, especially if the debt you owe is substantial. The mention of bankruptcy may motivate a debt collector to settle your unsecured debt for less than what you owe.

In the end, debt settlement may cause you to owe more in federal income taxes because the amount that you don't pay is reported to the IRS as income. However, depending on the state of your finances when you settle the debt, the IRS may decide that you are insolvent so you won't owe any federal taxes.[22]

My Settlement Experience

I once had a credit card that I wanted to create a settlement for which would have saved me approximately $250.00 from the original bill. Well, after a few telephone conversations, the creditor agreed to the settlement, however, when they refused to confirm this in writing, and started asking for my banking information; I opted NOT to go the settlement root. Instead, I paid a $50 a month until I paid off the entire bill. Granted, it took a little longer to pay off this bill, I however felt more in control of how this bill was paid. On the other hand, I had another creditor, for an OLD debt of $1522. Well, they accepted a plan of 4 months paying $209 per month for a total of $837. (SUCCESS)

List your thoughts (and plans) below:

_____
_____
_____
_____
_____
_____
_____
_____

---

[22] http://www.dummies.com/how-to/content/negotiating-a-debt-collection-settlement.html

Apps and Online Programs / Debt Management

Ok, let's admit it, people love their smartphones. So why not use them to help you track your debt free journey. Another method to stay abreast of your finances is to use a debt management program. Most of the following are free or affordable and simple to use. They will keep you accountable.

Paid Budgeting Apps
We don't often recommend spending money, but these apps may just be worth an exception. Occasionally, paying for something can actually save you money, such as budgeting apps. If a few dollars spent equals many dollars saved, we give it two thumbs up:

HomeBudget ($5.99 – 3.5 stars)
This is the app that we've used for a few years, and we continue to use it. If you're looking for an app that requires you to manually enter your income and expenses, this is a great option. The setup is easy, you can make your budget as comprehensive as you'd like (or not like), while keeping it uncomplicated. Our favorite feature is that the app syncs between our devices so we can keep each other in the loop on our expenditures in real time. It's not totally perfect, but as one reviewer put it, HomeBudget's the least bad money tracker out there.

Coinkeeper ($1.99/month – 4.5 stars)
Coinkeeper has a fun interface of dropping "coins" into different expenses. Much like the "envelope system," it's nice to actually watch your money move from your accounts to your various categories. Its light, clean, simple design makes it easy and enjoyable to use. You manually enter your planned expenses and income, and it's all visible in one place. The app is listed for free, but the premium (i.e., paid) option would be necessary for most to budget effectively. It is developed in Russia, so some of the text and labels in the app are lost in translation, but all in all, this is a very worthy app.

YNAB($5.00/month – 3 stars)

The latest and greatest version of YNAB (which stands for You Need A Budget) automatically imports your bank accounts and expenses, but you still create your custom budget. You use the phone app in companionship with the web app, which allows you to create a budget that's whole and comprehensive. And although your expenses are automatically imported, you still manually categorize and approve them so that you remain an active participant in your budgeting (which we're huge proponents of). As with HomeBudget, YNAB syncs between devices so you and your spouse/partner can stay up to date.

Free Budgeting Apps

You won't spend a dime on these apps, but they may save you lots and lots of dimes. If one of them sounds like it'll fit your current budgeting needs, go get that freebie right now:

BillGuard(4.5 stars)

Unlike the other two free apps listed below, Billguard automatically tracks your spending, rather than entering it manually. You simply add your accounts during setup and all of your expenditures will be imported for you. But what makes Billguard unique from other budgeting and personal finance apps of its kind is that you can review your expenses and approve them. And true to its name, Billguard alerts you of any suspicious or duplicate charges to help keep your finances safe as well. Whether you end up using this app for tracking your budget or not, it's worth downloading for this feature alone.

Dollarbird (4.5 stars)

This app is just a delight with its bright, simple design. This is a great option to get you started budgeting with just a few quick, easy steps. And the concept is simple: how much money you currently have versus how much you're spending. Their unique calendar-view approach makes it super easy to see an overview of how much you spend each day throughout the month.

Fudget(3.5 stars)

If you're looking for free and simple, Fudget is the budgeting app for you. They strip away all the bells and whistles and complexities of budgeting, but keep the meaty basics. This app helps you track your income and expenses and see where you stand, period. This is a great option *for budgeting beginners and minimalists alike who just need/want to get in the habit of tracking where your money goes each month.*

Free Savings Apps
We couldn't resist including this category this year since there are so many clever, effective apps for saving money. We've used (and still use) all three of these apps and would recommend each and every one:

Digit (free)
Digit automates your savings like a boss. It connects to your bank account, analyzes your spending, and then takes small amounts of money you don't need (usually between $5 and $50) and saves it for you. It then updates you via text and tells you how much it has socked away into savings for you each week. The entire "app" takes place via text messaging, so if you ever want to check your balance or withdraw/transfer some of those savings, you just have to send a text and you're on your way. We love how painless savings becomes with Digit.

Qapital(free – 4.5 stars)
Qapital helps you save by using rules, or more specifically IFTTT (if this then that) recipes. When one of the rules or goals you've set gets triggered by the recipe you've created (like completing a run with Nike+), money automatically gets saved. On the flip side, you can also have money taken away when you break rules you've set for yourself (like shopping at Target).

Acorns(free* – 4 stars)
Investing is no walk in the park, but Acorns makes it easy peasy. This app invests your spare change by rounding up your expenses to the nearest dollar and invests the extra into a diversified portfolio. It's completely automatic, and your money doesn't just get saved — it grows (assuming the markets are doing well). You can also deposit or withdraw your own specified amounts at any time. And while the app is technically free to download, once you start investing, it costs $1/month (but free if you're a student).

General Finance Apps

Just in case keeping a budget is merely whetting your financial appetite, we've listed some general finance apps that are super helpful in their own special way:

Personal Capital(free* – 4.5 stars)

If you like Mint, you'll love Personal Capital. If you're already investing and starting to save for retirement, you may use Personal Capital to simply track your money over time. You can view all your accounts and investments in one place, analyze your net worth, and set financial goals. You can also receive personalized help from their financial advisors anytime you need it. And while the app is completely free to use, they do charge a 0.89% fee on all assets that are actively managed.

Penny(free – 4.5 stars)

Penny is billed as a "personal finance coach." This clever app offers fun and useful insights about your spending, and it does so with a very personal interface. The entire experience happens via chat with "Penny," your money coach, who tracks your spending and income, shares facts about your spending habits, and helps you plan for the weeks and months ahead. Penny is like having your very own financial assistant/friend who will never give you up, let you down, run around or desert you. (thanks, Rick Astley)

Mint(free – 4.5 stars)

When it comes to tracking your finances, Mint is the pioneer and godfather of all the personal finance apps. And although you can create your own budget in the app, we steer clear of using it for this purpose for a number of reasons, including the annoyance that many transactions end up miscategorized. So while using it for budgeting can be more tedious than it should be at times, we absolutely love using it as a way to see an overview of our money. All of our accounts are listed, so we can easily see where we stand financially with a big-picture perspective. When we track our net worth at the end of each month, we always use Mint to get it done.[23]

---

[23] Http://www.ourfreakingbudget.com/best-budgeting-saving-apps-of-2016/

Saving (What is that?)

This is a tough chapter, so let's start it out with a little comedy.

Save - to avoid the spending, consumption, or waste of.

I'm sure that you have heard it before:
- I don't trust banks
- This money is already spent
- My money is burning hole in my pocket

Well there is actually a reason for this and after reading this section, you will understand why.

Freedman Banks

22 million reasons black America doesn't trust banks

"This bank is just what the freedmen need," remarked President Abraham Lincoln on March 3, 1865, as he signed the Freedman's Bank Act, authorizing the organization of a national bank for recently emancipated black Americans.
A little more than a month later he was killed, making the Freedman's Bank Lincoln's last act of emancipation.
His assassination, however, did not impede its rapid growth. By January 1874, less than ten years after the establishment of the Freedman's Bank, deposits at its 34 branches across the United States totaled US$3,299,201 ($65,200,000 in current dollars).
Despite such successful expansion, the Freedman's Bank closed on June 28, 1874 under a shroud of suspicion and accusation..[24]

Did I Get Your Attention Yet? It sure got mine. Throughout my life I heard stories about my Great Grandfather William Samuel-Salmon and his 'bag of money'. He carried around a brown paper bag of money full of money My great aunts, great uncles and older cousins always talked about this 'bag of money'. Well, I thought it was bazaar that this seemingly wise man would carry his money around in a bag, along with his shotgun. UNTIL, I learned of the Freeman's Bank.

Read the following story and you too will understand why a man born nearly 130 years ago didn't trust banks either …

History Explains Why Black Americans Don't Trust Banks
Reported by Liku Zelleke

The mistrust African-Americans have of financial institutions, especially banks, has been around for a long time. In fact, the uneasiness has been around ever since the 1800s when the first bank for Black people was established.

---

[24] http://www.washingtonsblog.com/2015/03/22-million-reasons-black-america-doesnt-trust-banks.html

It was Abraham Lincoln who signed the Freedman's Bank Act, allowing for the organization of a national bank for Black people who had recently gained their freedom. But it didn't fare too well. One of the reasons being that President Lincoln was assassinated less than a month after, costing many African-Americans their life savings.

Initially, the Freedman's Bank grew at a rapid pace — 34 branches were opened in 10 years and were worth more than $3 million. But then on June 26, 1874 it was shut down amid a controversy.

The United States Congress had just approved the bank six months before its demise. John W. Alvord, a white northerner, a former minister, and attaché to General William Tecumseh Sherman, was its first president. He went throughout the South to recruit blacks using endorsements from General Howard by saying, "...as an order from Howard... Negro soldiers should deposit their bounty money with him."

The bank became a siphon that would take the savings and incomes of blacks to be used for the betterment of whites and pretty soon corruption followed, which in turn led to the bank's management being replaced with a series of black elites.

One such elite, Frederick Douglas, who was appointed head of the bank in 1874, would compare his experience as being unwittingly "married to a corpse."

When the end came, black clients of the bank would lose about $22 million in today's adjusted currency and even by 1900, only 62% ($1,638,259.49) of that money would ever be returned to them.

Fast forward to today and things still don't seem too bright. At present, there are only 19 black-owned banks in the US and about 70% of them are struggling to stay afloat. The success of such institutions is a must for black advancement, but the aftershocks of that first bank's collapse still seem to reverberate.

As W.E.B. Du Bois puts it, "Then in one sad day came the crash—all the hard-earned dollars of the freedmen disappeared; but that was the least of the loss—all the faith in saving went too, and much of the faith in men; and that was a loss that a nation which to-day sneers at Negro shiftlessness has never yet made good."

Booker T. Washington also agrees, "When they found out that they had lost, or been swindled out of all their savings, they lost faith in savings banks, and it was a long time after this before it was possible to mention a savings bank for Negroes without some reference being made to the disaster of [the Freedmen's Bank]." [25]

I debated as to whether or not I would add this final article because I didn't want to sound redundant, however this last article had a wealth of valuable information that I had to include it.

The REAL Reason Why Blacks Spend Their Money and Don't Save

As the largest racial minority in the United States, blacks make up approximately 13.2% of the population, but have a spending power of over one-trillion dollars. So why is it that blacks have the lowest net worth of all racial classes?

During the Civil War, small banks were established throughout the country to be financially responsible for freed and runaway slaves' deposits. However, many of those individuals lost their money because the banks "lost" their deposits. And after the Civil War, blacks had practically no economic resources, access to capital, or entrepreneurial abilities, making it almost impossible to build, accrue, and pass on wealth. But in an attempt to financially assist soldiers and emancipated slaves with transitioning into "freedom," Congress established the Freedman's Savings and Trust Company - a financial institution for blacks. The bank's objective was to help blacks "increase their financial strength."

With the assistance of the bank, the black economy grew, allowing hospitals, churches, small businesses, charities, schools, and other organizations to open and flourish. Ultimately, the bank had 37 branches in 17 states. However, because money was stolen and poorly invested by the bank's upper management and board of directors, it failed. And unfortunately, the FDIC didn't exist during that time, and therefore, blacks lost all of their money.

---

[25] http://financialjuneteenth.com/history-explains-why-black-americans-dont-trust-banks/

This historic fact has aided, abetted, and perpetuated the attitudes and financial customs of black people today. In the 21st century, many blacks still don't possess bank accounts, but instead rely on check cashing services, prepaid debit cards, and those alike. And living an "all cash" lifestyle allows for more spending and less saving. However, because of the history of being financially defrauded, blacks have grown to rely on tangible items to justify their finances. In other words, many of them feel more secure being able to see and spend their money instead of trusting a financial institution. Consequently, the more items bought and the more expensive items may be, signifies many blacks' interpretation of their net worth and status as opposed to what a savings account may indicate.

To add fuel to the fire, banks haven't attempted to improve their broken relationship with blacks by redlining. To the date, loan process lenders are avoiding to offer mortgage services to low and middle-income black areas and charge higher mortgage interest rates to blacks than they would whites in those neighborhoods. These discriminatory practices only makes it virtually impossible for blacks to use their income to purchase properties, land, and businesses.

Studies have shown that managing: household expenses and budget, money and debt, investments, and to save for college education are areas that many blacks aren't financially literate. This fact is attributable to African-American's poor financial experiences and history. Long-term financial planning, personal debt, and how to increase engagement with financial professionals aren't financial realms in which many black families are believed to be knowledgeable. However, to say many doesn't mean all.

Approach to Money Among African Americans
(Percentage among all respondents)

Total
40% Spender
51% Saver
9% Investor

Well-Prepared for Financial Decisions
29% Spender
59% Saver
11% Investor

Not Well-Prepared for Financial Decisions
52% Spender
42% Saver
6% Investor

Data provided by Prudential Research
In a 2013 survey, Prudential Research reported that 40% of blacks considered themselves to be spenders, 51% savers, and only 9% that actually invest. Furthermore, 54% of African-Americans believe that their "overall financial situation is better than that of their parents when they were their age, that their own financial situation is better now than it was five years ago, and that they believe the next generation of their family will have a better financial situation than their own."

Despite where blacks "consider" themselves to be in the financial spectrum, reports provided by the Census Bureau shows that blacks have the lowest net worth of all racial classes. This is primarily attributable to the fact that they were robbed of the many privileges naturally warranted to whites.

To this date, blacks only possess 5% of America's wealth, oppose to whites that own 61%, Asians 28%, and Hispanics 6%.

Therefore, the real reason why blacks spend their money and don't save is because systematic racism prevented them from safely investing in banks, and is currently impacting their ability to own property, land, or businesses, thus leaving them with nothing to pass down to future generations. They were forced into a mindset of poverty–spend now before it's gone, impacting them generationally. Historical experiences blinded African-Americans from recognizing the importance of financial literacy and because of their monetary ignorance, blacks possess the least amount of wealth in America.[26]

[26] http://racisminamerica.org/the-real-reason-why-blacks-spend-their-money-and-dont-save/

Ways to Save Money

It's not always how much money you make, but it is always about how much money you keep. Spend Less.

Growing up in my family house, during the winter, I always felt like my bedroom was a little drafty, however when I would turn up the heat in the house, my father would fuss at me and tell me "don't touch that thermostat, put on a sweater." Well, it wasn't until I was older and responsible for my own utility bills did I truly understand why he was fussing. Those bills can get HIGH unless you have some control. So yes, one of the methods that I use to maintain a low utility bill is to wear really warm clothes when the weather is cold outside. Of course, you will also want to winterized your home. And during the summer time I did the opposite, I keep windows open to allow for a breeze to circulate and if it gets excessively hot, take a trip to the Mall to enjoy their ac. (wink).

Need more money saving ideas? Check out the following list:

54 Ways to save Money

Build an emergency fund. *It can make all the difference. Low-income families with at least $500 in an emergency fund are better off financially than moderate-income families with less saved up.*

Establish your budget. *Are you looking for an easy way to begin? On the first day of a new month, get a receipt for everything you purchase. Stack the receipts into categories like restaurants, groceries, and personal care. At the end of the month you will be able to clearly see where your money is going.*

Budget with cash and envelopes. *If you have trouble with overspending, try the envelope budget system where you use a set amount of cash for most spending. And once the cash is gone, it's gone.*

Don't just save money, save. *There's a difference between saving money and saving money for your future. So don't just spend less, put the money you save into a savings account to plan for college expenses, retirement, or emergencies that can leave you financially better off.*

Save automatically *Setting up automatic savings is the easiest and most effective way to save, and it puts extra cash out of sight and out of mind. Every pay period, have your employer deduct a certain amount from your paycheck and transfer it to a retirement or savings account. Ask your HR representative for more details about how to set this up. Or every month, have your bank or credit union transfer a fixed amount from your checking account to a savings or investment account.*

Aim for short-term savings goals. *Make a goal such as setting aside $20 a week or month, rather than a longer term savings goal. People save more successfully when they keep short-term goals in sight.*

Start saving for your retirement as early as possible. *Few people get rich through their wages alone. It's the miracle of compound interest, or earning interest on your interest over many years, that builds wealth. Because time is on their side, the youngest workers are in the best position to save for retirement.*

Take full advantage of employer matches to your retirement plan. *Often as an incentive, employers will match a certain amount of what you save in a retirement plan such as a 401(k). If you don't take full advantage of this match, you're leaving money on the table.*

Save your windfalls and tax refunds. *Every time you receive a windfall, such a work bonus, inheritance, contest winnings, or tax refund, put a portion into your savings account.*

Make a savings plan. *Those with a savings plan are twice as likely to save successfully. That's where America Saves comes in. If you take the America Saves Pledge, we'll help you set a goal and make a plan. And it doesn't stop there. America Saves will keep you motivated with information, advice, tips, and reminders to help you reach your savings goal. Think of us as your own personal support system.*

Save your loose change. *Really! Putting aside just 50¢ over a year will get you 40 percent of the way to a $500 emergency fund. And some banks and credit unions or apps offer programs that round all your purchases to the nearest dollar and put that money into a separate savings account.*

Use the 24 hour rule. *This rules helps avoid purchasing expensive or unnecessary items on impulse. Think over each nonessential purchase for at least 24 hours. This is particularly easy to do while shopping online, because you can add items to your cart or wish list and come back to them a day later.*

Treat yourself, but use it as an opportunity to save. *Match the cost of your nonessential indulgences in savings. So, for example, if you splurge on a smoothie while out running errands, put the same amount into your savings account. And think of it this way, if you can't afford to save the matching amount, you can't afford the treat either.*

Calculate purchases by hours worked instead of cost. *Take the amount of the item you're considering purchasing and divide it by your hourly wage. If it's a $50 pair of shoes and you make $10 an hour, ask yourself if those shoes are really worth five long hours of work.*

Unsubscribe. *Avoid temptation by unsubscribing from marketing emails to the stores you spend the most money at. By law, each email is required to have an unsubscribe link, usually at the bottom of the email.*

Place a savings reminder on your card. *Remind yourself to think through every purchase by covering your card with a savings message, such as "Do I really need this?" Write the message on a piece of masking tape or colorful washi tape on your card.*

Participate in a local Investment Development Account (or IDA) program. *If your income is low, you may be eligible to participate in an IDA program where your savings are matched. In return for attending financial education sessions and planning to save for a home, education, or business, you typically receive at least $1 for every $1 you save, and sometimes much more. That means $25 saved each month could become several hundred dollars by the end of the year.*

Banking, Credit, and Debt Savings Tips

Pay off credit cards in full each month. *The miles and cash-back are only valuable if you're not falling into debt or paying interest.*

Start with a goal of reducing your credit card debt by just $1,000. *That $1,000 debt reduction will probably save you $150-200 a year in interest, and much more if you're paying penalty rates of 20-30 percent.*

Use only the ATMs of your bank or credit union. *Using the ATM of another financial institution once a week might seem like no big deal, but if it's costing you $3 for each withdrawal, that's more than $150 over the course of a year.*

Check your credit report for free once a year. *Use your annual free credit report from the three credit reporting bureaus to look for inaccuracies or opportunities to raise your score. Credit scores are used by loan providers, landlords, and others to determine what they'll sell you, and at what price. For example, a low credit score can increase the cost of a 60-month, $20,000 auto loan by more than $5,000.*

Pay all of your bills on auto-pay. *This ensures they are paid on time, in full to avoid late charges. As a bonus, some loan providers offer a small interest rate deduction if you enroll in auto-pay.*

Get free debt counseling. *The most widely available help managing your debt is with a Consumer Credit Counseling Services (CCCS) counselor. CCCS' network of non-profit counselors can work with you confidentially and judgement-free to help you develop a budget, figure out your options, and negotiate with creditors to repay your debts. Best of all, the 45-90 minute counseling sessions are free of charge and come with no obligations. Get started here.*

Freeze your credit, literally. *If you are having trouble controlling your credit card use, but don't want to cut up your credit card in case you need it at some point, freeze your credit card in a bag of water. Needing to thaw your card will force you to really consider the purchase before you make it.*

Entertainment Savings Tips

Take advantage of your library. *More and more libraries are offering e-books, so you don't even need to visit in person. Many libraries are also part of an intra-library loan system where you can borrow anything you want, but that they don't have, for a minimal shipping charge. Just ask. And some libraries allow you to borrow things like tools and sewing machines.*

Get unadvertised theater ticket discounts. *Call, email, or tweet your nearby theater to ask about discount options that are often not well-advertised. Many theaters offer discounted seats for seniors, students, and young adults, such as pay-your-age or pay-what-you-can programs. Or they'll offer rush discounts of any unsold seats immediately before a show.*

Volunteer at local festivals. *Cultural festivals and events often offer free admission to event volunteers. Contact the organizers of your favorite event to ask about volunteer opportunities and benefits.*

Family and Friends Savings Tips

Create a family spending limit on gifts. *Discuss placing spending limits on gifts within your family and/or a system where you only purchase one gift for one person over the holidays. These limits tend to reduce expenditures and be greatly appreciated by family members with less financial flexibility.*

Plan gift-giving well in advance. *That will give you time to decide on the most thoughtful gifts, which usually are not the most expensive ones. And if these gifts are products that must be purchased, you will have the opportunity to look for sales.*

Start saving for college at the baby shower. *It's never too soon to start a college savings account for junior. Ask for contributions to a college fund instead of clothing and toy gifts for your new baby.*

Don't buy cheap clothes for cheap's sake. *It sometimes make sense to prioritize quality over price when purchasing clothes for the family. An inexpensive shirt or coat is a poor bargain for older family members if it wears out in less than a year, but could make sense for quickly growing children. Consider fabric, stitching, washability, and other quality related factors in your selection of clothes.*

Organize a neighborhood swap meet. *Here's how it works: gather your friends and neighbors with kids around the same age and everyone brings gently used clothing, books, and school supplies, toys, etc., and receives a ticket for each item they bring. Each ticket entitles you to one item from the swap meet. If you contribute six books, you can leave with up to six new-to-you books. If you contribute seven items of clothing, you can leave with up to seven new-to-you items of clothing. All leftover items are donated.*

Designate one day a week a "no spend day." *Reserve one night a week for free family fun. Cook at home, and plan out free activities such as game night, watching a movie, or going to the park.*

Food Savings Tips

Brown bag your lunch. *The reason you hear this tip so much is that it works! If buying lunch at work costs $5, but making lunch at home costs only $2.50, then in a year, you could afford to create a $500 emergency fund and still have money left over.*

Commit to eating out one fewer time each month. *Save money without sacrificing your lifestyle by taking small steps to reduce your dining budget. Start off with reducing the amount you eat out by just once per month.*

Plan your meals in advance and stick to a list while grocery shopping. *People who do food shopping with a list, and buy little else, spend much less money than those who decide what to buy when they get to the food market. The annual savings could easily be hundreds of dollars.*

Shop by unit price. *Many grocery stores list a cost per unit of each item, such as the price per ounce or pound. Use these stickers when comparison shopping for the same product, just in a different size.*

Stick to water. *It's standard in the restaurant industry to mark up the cost of alcohol by three to five times. So an easy way to cut down on your restaurant spending without changing your habits too drastically is to skip the beverages, alcoholic and non-alcoholic.*

Save time and money by doubling the recipe. *Next time you make a family favorite, double the recipe and freeze the leftovers for another day. That way you can get two meals out of one and use the ingredients more efficiently with less waste. Aluminum pans of various sizes can be purchased on the cheap, especially when buying bulk, and make freezing and reheating a snap.*

Health Savings Tips

Don't skimp on preventive healthcare. *Routine dental checkups, for example, help prevent fillings, root canals, and dental crowns, which are expensive and no fun.*

Go generic. *Ask your physician if generic prescription drugs are a good option for you. Generic drugs can cost several hundred dollars less to purchase annually than brand-name drugs. And since physicians often don't know the costs you incur for a particular drug, you often have to ask.*

Comparison shop for prescription drugs. *Don't just rely on the closest drugstore because the cost to you can vary significantly from pharmacy to pharmacy. Make sure to check out your local pharmacist, supermarkets, wholesale clubs, and mail-order pharmacies.*

Purchase store brand over-the-counter medications. *Store brand medications often cost 20-40 percent less than nationally advertised brands, but are the exact same formula. The premium you're paying on brand names is for nothing but the marketing.*

Home Savings Tips

Comparison shop for homeowners insurance. *Before renewing your existing homeowners insurance policy each year, check out the rates of competing companies.*

Refinance your mortgage. *Explore if you have the option to refinance your mortgage to a lower interest rate. On a 15-year $100,000 fixed-rate mortgage, lowering the rate from 7 percent to 6.5 percent can save you more than $5,000 in interest charges over the life of the loan. And, you will accumulate home equity more rapidly, thus increasing your ability to cover large emergency expenditures.*

Audit your home energy use. *Ask your local electric or gas utility for a free or low-cost home energy audit. The audit may reveal inexpensive ways to reduce home heating and cooling costs by hundreds of dollars a year. Keep in mind that a payback period of less than three years, or even five years, usually will save you lots of money in the long-term.*

Weatherproof your home. *Caulk holes and cracks that let warm air escape in the winter and cold air escape in the summer. Your local hardware store has materials, and quite possibly useful advice, about inexpensively stopping unwanted heat or cooling loss.*

Keep the sun out. *Keep your blinds or curtains closed during hot summer days. Blocking the sunlight really does help to keep your house cooler.*

Use less water. *Install low-flow showerheads and faucet aerators to reduce your water usage and water costs.*

Cut laundry detergent and dryer sheet use in half. *The laundry detergent sold today is usually highly concentrated and powerful. Use the smallest suggested amount, and often you can use less than what's on the bottle and still get clean clothes. In many cases, using less actually washes more effectively because there's no leftover soap in your clothes. And tearing your dryer sheets in half gives the same result for half the price.*

Lower the temperature on your water heater to 120 degrees. *For every 10 degree reduction in temperature, you can save up to 5 percent on water heating costs.*

Transportation Savings Tips

Comparison shop for auto insurance. *Before renewing your existing auto insurance policy each year, check out the rates of competing companies.*

Invest in car maintenance. *Keeping your car engine tuned and its tires inflated to their proper pressure saves money in the long run. Doing both can save you up to $100 a year in gas.*

Check multiple sites for low airfares. *Don't rely on a single airline search engine to show you all inexpensive fares. Some discount carriers do not allow their flights to be listed in these third-party searches, so you need to check their websites separately.* [27]

How to Eat To Live

One of the quickest ways to save money is to stop eating out and start cooking all your meals at home and meal planning is a critical part of cooking at home.

When I first started paying down debt; I was determined to spend only $30 a week on food purchases. The first week was a complete bust, mostly because I was not organized with what I was going to eat. Looking back at that week, I won't say that I was hungry, but I will say that I was constantly looking in the refrigerator for leftovers.

---

[27] https://americasaves.org/for-savers/make-a-plan-how-to-save-money/54-ways-to-save-money

The following article details the steps needed to meal plan properly:

Meal Planning

A Step-By-Step Guide to Grocery Store Savings

Step 1: Get a Flyer and Print Coupons
The most important step is to check around for ongoing deals and coupons on the products you're looking to buy. Get a flyer from your grocery store – or perhaps flyers from two or three local grocery stores and look for online manufacturers coupons. The Simple Dollar Coupon Finder has hundreds of daily coupons and coupon codes that you simply save and print, providing you with extra savings on your trip to the grocery store.

Step 2: Find Sales on Fresh Ingredients
Once I have the flyers, I go through them and mark any sales on fresh ingredients that they have. For example, as I write this, I'm reviewing Hy-Vee's ad for October 14 through October 20, and I'm noticing several things on sale: fresh zucchini for $0.89 a pound, fresh yellow squash for $0.89 a pound, sweet yellow onions for $0.99 a pound, yellow bell peppers for $0.99 a pound, tons of apple sales, ground turkey for $2.18 a pound, hormone- and antibiotic-free cageless chicken for $1.99 a pound, and so on.
I ignore the sales on most prepackaged items. We focus on buying fresh foods and staples like flour for our meals. Over the long haul, the fresh items are cheaper and healthier.

Step 3: Do Some Recipe Research
This week, I know I'll be working with ground turkey, whole chicken, zucchini and squash, yellow bell peppers, sweet yellow onions, apples, and the other meat we have in our freezer from bulk purchases. What recipes can I find that utilize these ingredients?

I go to a recipe search engine like FoodieView and just enter combinations of the on-sale fresh ingredients that sound interesting. My first attempt was searching for "turkey, zucchini, onion" and I immediately found a turkey and zucchini meat loaf recipe from Epicurious. Searching for *"yellow bell, chicken"* gets me an interesting chicken bell pepper recipe (which I'll use, but modify a bit). Chicken-apple-bacon burgers? Yum. Plus, you can easily grill sliced squash (dipped in olive oil and ground pepper) for a wonderful vegetable side dish.

These ideas provide the backbone for several meals throughout the week, so I start planning ahead.

Step 4: Create a Week-Long Meal Plan

I usually start off with my blank meal-planning worksheet and fill in the dinners first based on the above recipes. For us, breakfasts are usually quite simple and lunches usually consist of leftovers, so those columns are quite easy as well.

I usually try to make most weeknight meals pretty easy. I usually attempt one difficult recipe during the week and one on a weekend, with the others being simple. Whole chicken roasting? That's a difficult one. Chicken-apple burgers? Easy.

We usually have homemade pizza one night a week, often Fridays. We also often have pasta one night a week, often Tuesdays (for some reason). So I'll pencil those things in, too. We have plenty of ingredients on hand for both, so I don't really need to shop for them – buying flour in bulk makes crust easy, and we keep tons of tomato sauce and ground beef on hand at all times.

Given all that, it's pretty easy to fill in the rest of the squares on that meal plan. I usually only need to come up with five suppers per week and two to three lunches per week (for meals where leftovers from the night before don't carry over). Often, these are just simple sandwiches.

Step 5: Make a Shopping List from the Meal Plan

Once the meal plan is in place, I go through and list all of the ingredients for all of the recipes I'll make and then cross off the things we have as I find them in the cupboards or refrigerator. Most of this is very easy, but it saves us money – we don't accidentally buy things we already have on hand.

I also check the staples – flour, milk, yeast, juice boxes, and so on – and add replenishments to the list.

Step 6: Go Grocery Shopping – And Stick to Your List

Once you have the list in place, it's simple. Take it to the grocery store and stick to it. Don't toss stuff that's not on your list into the cart. Since you've already planned your meals, you know that you don't need it.

Using this path will also make grocery shopping itself substantially quicker. Most of your purchases will be around the edges of the store, in the produce and meat sections. You won't have to go up and down every aisle to find the items you need. This will shave significant time off of your shopping trip.

In the end, though, when you go home, unpack your groceries, and put that meal plan up on the fridge, you'll find that overall it hasn't taken you any more time than a grocery trip without planning would have taken, plus you now have a clear plan for meals for the week and you've saved significant money at the grocery store.

Good luck![28]

---

[28] http://www.thesimpledollar.com/how-to-plan-ahead-for-next-weeks-meals-ad-save-significant-money-a-step-by-step-guide/

Now that you have read how to meal plan, here is an example of one of my previous Monthly Meal Plans

Sunday	Monday	Tuesday	Wednesday	Thursday	Friday	Saturday
Traditional Meals	**Asian/Indian**	**Healthy**	**Caribbean, Mexican**	**Beans & Rice**	**Italian & Re-Runs**	**Eating Out / Re-Runs**
	1 General Tso Chicken over Rice	2 Bean Soup and Grill Cheese	3 Seitan Tacos & Vegetables	4 Baked Beans, Hot Dogs over Rice	5 Spinach Calzones	6 Red Navy Bean Chili w/ toppings
7 Vegetable Pot Pies	8 Pad Thai	9 Salmon Patties, Rice& Cabbage	10 Bean & Cheese Burritos	11 Lentil Stew over Rice w/Broccoli	12 Lasagna	13 Planned Dinner Out
14 Meatloaf, Potatoes, Mac & Cheese	15 Chicken & Broccoli, Eggrolls	16 White Navy Bean Chili w/ toppings	17 Cheese Enchiladas, Beans, Spicy Corn	18 Red Beans & Butternut over Rice	19 Pizza w/ toppings	20 Homemade Burgers & Onion Rings
21 Leftover Lasagna	22 Tandori Fish & Curried Vegetables	23 Creamy Beans & Sandwiches	24 Jerk Chicken, Peas&Rice, Plantains	25 BBQ Beans w/ Seitan, Corn & BBQ Chicken	26 Vegetable Pizza w/ Creamy Beans	27 Breakfast for Dinner
28 Spaghetti & Meatballs	29 Potstickers & Vegetable Fried Rice	30 French Onion Soup & Salad	31			

You will notice that I only have a chart for dinner, that I am not big on Breakfast and Lunch. In addition to the health benefits, eating less is also a huge saver of money. Why not take a week or two to try it yourself.

If you must have three meals a day, here is a sample of chart that you can use.

	BREAKFAST	LUNCH	SNACK	DINNER
M				
T				
W				
TH				
F				
SA				
SU				

Bobby Joe's Saving Method

As a savings plan, my father always opened several yearly Christmas accounts.

*The **Christmas club** is a savings program that was first offered by various banks in the United States during the Great Depression. The concept is that bank customers deposit a set amount of money each week into a special savings **account**, and receive the money back at the end of the year for **Christmas** shopping.*[29]

He kept account for all three children and an extra one for himself so that he had some pocket money during the month of December. The interesting thing is that there was never a surprise about what you were going to get from him for Christmas. The only surprise was when were you going to get the money. (smile)

Though most banks no longer offer this service, there are still a few that do. And the same way that my father maintained his Christmas accounts, creating other accounts are possible. Maybe a Staycation or Vacation accounts. Simply save the money each week in a jar with a **DON'T TOUCH** sign attached to it.

Once you determine the type of account that you would like to fund, calculate how much money you will need for it to be fully funded. For example, if you want a vacation fund add the costs for:

Travel to your destination
Transportation while you're there
Accommodations
Food and drink
Must-do activities (for example, the Broadway show that made you decide to visit New York in the first place)
Discretionary spending (for unexpected expenses and impulse purchases)

---

[29] *https://en.wikipedia.org/wiki/**Christmas_club***

Once you have figured out your total expenses, then you can use the following chart to see how much you will need to save each week.

*Note – this chart includes $1 a week savings to teach your children how to save.

Weekly Amount	$1.00	$2.00	$5.00	$10.00	$15.00	$25.00	$100.00
Week1	$1	$2.00	$5.00	$10.00	$15.00	$25.00	$100.00
Week2	$2	$4.00	$10.00	$20.00	$30.00	$50.00	$200.00
Week3	$3	$6.00	$15.00	$30.00	$45.00	$75.00	$300.00
Week4	$4	$8.00	$20.00	$40.00	$60.00	$100.00	$400.00
Week5	$5	$10.00	$25.00	$50.00	$75.00	$125.00	$500.00
Week6	$6	$12.00	$30.00	$60.00	$90.00	$150.00	$600.00
Week7	$7	$14.00	$35.00	$70.00	$105.00	$175.00	$700.00
Week8	$8	$16.00	$40.00	$80.00	$120.00	$200.00	$800.00
Week9	$9	$18.00	$45.00	$90.00	$135.00	$225.00	$900.00
Week10	$10	$20.00	$50.00	$100.00	$150.00	$250.00	$1000.00
Week11	$11	$22.00	$55.00	$110.00	$165.00	$275.00	$1100.00
Week12	$12	$24.00	$60.00	$120.00	$180.00	$300.00	$1200.00
Week13	$13	$26.00	$65.00	130.00	$195.00	$325.00	$1300.00
Week14	$14	$28.00	$70.00	140.00	$210.00	$350.00	$1400.00
Week15	$15	$30.00	$75.00	150.00	$225.00	$375.00	$1500.00
Week16	$16	$32.00	$80.00	160.00	$240.00	$400.00	$1600.00
Week17	$17	$34.00	$85.00	170.00	$255.00	$425.00	$1700.00
Week18	$18	$36.00	$90.00	180.00	$270.00	$450.00	$1800.00
Week19	$19	$38.00	$95.00	190.00	$285.00	$475.00	$1900.00
Week20	$20	$40.00	$100.00	200.00	$300.00	$500.00	$2000.00
Week21	$21	$42.00	$105.00	210.00	$315.00	$525.00	$2100.00
Week22	$22	$44.00	$110.00	220.00	$330.00	$550.00	$2200.00
Week23	$23	$46.00	$115.00	230.00	$345.00	$575.00	$2300.00
Week24	$24	$48.00	$120.00	240.00	$360.00	$600.00	$2400.00
Week25	$25	$50.00	$125.00	250.00	$375.00	$625.00	$2500.00
Week26	$26	$52.00	$130.00	260.00	$390.00	$650.00	$2600.00
Week27	$27	$54.00	$135.00	270.00	$405.00	$675.00	$2700.00
Week28	$28	$56.00	$140.00	280.00	$420.00	$700.00	$2800.00
Week29	$29	$58.00	$145.00	290.00	$435.00	$725.00	$2900.00

Week30	$30	$60.00	$150.00	300.00	$450.00	$750.00	$3000.00
Week31	$31	$62.00	$155.00	$310.00	$465.00	$775.00	$3100.00
Week32	$32	$64.00	$160.00	$320.00	$480.00	$800.00	$3200.00
Week33	$33	$66.00	$165.00	$330.00	$495.00	$825.00	$3300.00
Week34	$34	$68.00	$170.00	$340.00	$510.00	$850.00	$3400.00
Week35	$35	$70.00	$175.00	$350.00	$525.00	$875.00	$3500.00
Week36	$36	$72.00	$180.00	$360.00	$540.00	$900.00	$3600.00
Week37	$37	$74.00	$185.00	$370.00	$555.00	$925.00	$3700.00
Week38	$38	$76.00	$190.00	$380.00	$570.00	$950.00	$3800.00
Week39	$39	$78.00	$195.00	$390.00	$585.00	$975.00	$3900.00
Week40	$40	$80.00	$200.00	$400.00	$600.00	$1000.00	$4000.00
Week41	$41	$82.00	$205.00	$410.00	$615.00	$1025.00	$4100.00
Week42	$42	$84.00	$210.00	$420.00	$630.00	$1050.00	$4200.00
Week43	$43	$86.00	$215.00	$430.00	$645.00	$1075.00	$4300.00
Week44	$44	$88.00	$220.00	$440.00	$660.00	$1100.00	$4400.00
Week45	$45	$90.00	$225.00	$450.00	$675.00	$1125.00	$4500.00
Week46	$46	$92.00	$230.00	$460.00	$690.00	$1150.00	$4600.00
Week47	$47	$94.00	$235.00	$470.00	$705.00	$1175.00	$4700.00
Week48	$48	$96.00	$240.00	$480.00	$720.00	$1200.00	$4800.00
Week49	$49	$98.00	$245.00	$490.00	$735.00	$1225.00	$4900.00
Week50	$50	$100.00	$250.00	$500.00	$750.00	$1250.00	$5000.00
Week51	$51	$102.00	$255.00	$510.00	$765.00	$1275.00	$5100.00
Week52	$52	$104.00	$260.00	$520.00	$780.00	$1300.00	$5200.00
Total	$52.00	$104.00	$260.00	$520.00	$780.00	$1300.00	$5200.00

Most people live paycheck to paycheck

Recently while working as an independent contractor in a school, I noticed that my check was incorrect; it was short a few hours. I mentioned it to the owner of the business, and she was extremely apologetic, offering to bring the new check over to my home after work hours. I looked at her, smiled and stated, "I don't live paycheck to paycheck. Just cut me a new check on Monday and I will pick it up next week." She was stunned and I was a cool as a cucumber. The moral of this story is, had I not been on this debt free journey and planned in advance I probably would have been very stressed out. At that moment, I felt accomplished.

Who lives paycheck-to-paycheck? You might be surprised

Living hand-to-mouth -- or paycheck-to-paycheck -- is all too common for U.S. workers, three-quarters of whom scramble to cover their living costs.

Whether it's poor budget skills, the slow-growing economy or the fact that paychecks have been expanding at an anemic rate for much of the recovery, 38 percent of the more than 3,200 full-time workers nationwide who took part in an online survey said they sometimes live paycheck to paycheck. Another 15 percent said they usually get by this way and 23 percent said they always do, according to findings released Thursday by job-search firm CareerBuilder.

Conducted from May 11 to June 7 by Harris Poll, more than 2,100 full-time hiring and human resource managers in the private sector also participated in the survey.

Not surprisingly, those earning the least tend to live closest to the edge. Of workers who currently have a minimum-wage job or have held one in the past, 66 percent said they couldn't make ends meet, and 50 percent said they had to work more than one job to do so.

But just paying the bills isn't difficult only for low-income workers. A significant swath of Americans -- 19 percent -- at all salary levels said they weren't able to make ends meet every month last year.

Nine percent of those earning $100,000 or more each year felt they usually or always live paycheck-to-paycheck, while 23 percent of those making between $50,000 and $99,999 also *described living paycheck-to-paycheck, and 51 percent of those earning less than $50,000 met the description.*

Whether Americans at large are feeling pinched as a result of weak pay growth is difficult to say, with wage growth during much of the recovery averaging just above 2 percent.

If that's the case, however, the picture is brightening, with the latest monthly jobs report offering further positive evidence on the wages front. The July numbers had average hourly earnings rising 8 cents, or 0.3 percent, to $25.69, with annualized wages up 2.6 percent, the strongest increase since the recession ended in June of 2009.

Relatedly, just 5 percent of employers found the federal minimum wage of $7.25 an hour, which has remained the same for seven years, to be fair, according to CareerBuilder. A large majority -- 67 percent -- believe a fair minimum wage would be 10 bucks or more an hour, up from 61 percent last year.

Another 15 percent said a fair minimum wage would be $15 or more an hour, up from 11 percent in 2015. And 64 percent of employers believe the minimum wage should be increased in their state, up from 62 percent in 2014.

"Fair wages and benefits such as paid sick days are a hot political topic right now, and they're also on employers' minds," Rosemary Haefner, chief human resources officer for CareerBuilder, said in a statement accompanying the survey results.

Efforts to raise the federal minimum wage have become a national movement, dubbed Fight for $15. In May, the U.S. Supreme Court also refused to hear a challenge to Seattle's recent move to boost the base wage for employers in the city to $15 an hour. Several other cities and a group of states, including California and New York, have started to phase in a $15 minimum wage in recent months as the cost of living keeps rising.

The average full-time minimum-wage worker's annual earnings comes to $14,500, according to the Obama administration, which supports proposed legislation that would bring the federal minimum wage to $12 an hour by 2020.

CareerBuilder's poll found that even though most employers feel a fair minimum wage is $10 or more an hour, of those hiring minimum-wage workers this year, nearly half -- 48 percent -- said they're going to pay less than $10.[30]

---

[30] http://www.cbsnews.com/news/who-lives-paycheck-to-paycheck-you-might-be-surprised/

Stop Living Paycheck To Paycheck

The first thing that I did was to get ahead on my fixed monthly bills. Please note, this does not work with Credit Cards, as it will simply lower your balance and not be applied to the next month's payment. So I started out very small and slow with an extra $10. In your current budget, factor in an extra $5 or $10 towards **EACH** monthly fixed bill. Because my budget was very tight in the beginning, I was only able to target one bill at a time. I was able to add $10.00 per month. Look at the chart below.

My Monthly Fixed Bills
Gas - $40.00
Electricity - $50.00
Wifi - $60.00
AT&T – 80.00

Starting with the $40.00 a month Gas bill, for 4 months, instead of paying $40.00, I paid $50. When this bill was paid one month in advance, again this took 4 months to achieve a receive a zero balance, I returned to paying $40 a month. On month 5, I was actually a month in advance and then I always received a zero due statement.

Gas Bill

	Amount due	Amount paid
January Bill	$40.00	$50.00
February Bill	$30.00	$50.00
March Bill	$20.00	$50.00
April Bill	$10.00	$50.00
May Bill	$00.00	$40.00

I then moved to the next bill, which was Electricity and paid an extra $10 for 5 months until it was paid one month in advance, with a zero balance statement. Next was Wifi, followed by AT&T. Following this simple plan within 18 months I was 1 month ahead on all of my monthly bills.

List one of your bills and practice paying it down until its paid 1 month in advance.

	Amount due	Amount paid
January Bill	$	$
February Bill	$	$
March Bill	$	$
April Bill	$	$
May Bill	$	$
June Bill	$	$
July Bill	$	$
August Bill	$	$
September Bill	$	$
October Bill	$	$
November Bill	$	$
December Bill	$	$

Getting 13 Mortgage /Rent Payments out of 12 Months' Salary (Half Payments)

There are 12 months in a year however; there are 52 weeks, which means that if you are paid every other week; you need to pay 13 months' worth of mortgage, of get one month ahead in your rent. And to be truthful, it's not actually getting ahead, it really is applying extra money to your principle.

Ok, so let's do a little Mathematics. 52 (total weeks in a year) divided by 4(weeks in a month) = 13. Are you scratching your head yet? ☺ You know those 2 months during the year that you receive 3 paychecks instead of 2, well using this system, those 2 extra paychecks will become your 13th payment (or extra money to get ahead on a rent payment or, to knock out a different debt) Instead of paying your rent or mortgage monthly, divide the rent/mortgage payment amount in half.

Using this method, it will take a full 13 months to get 1 month ahead; HOWEVER, the wonderful side to this plan is that it can be used on ALL of your fixed bills. Picture yourself being able to have a little breathing room from the paycheck to paycheck struggle in just over 365 days???!!!

Family Mortgage (monthly) = $750

Paycheck #	Amount Applied	Month Applied To
Check #1 (1/8/16)	$375 (1/2 half of rent)	
Check #2 (1/22/16)	$750	January
Check #3	$375 (1/2 half of rent)	
Check #4	$750	February
Check #5	$375 (1/2 half of rent)	
Check #6	$750	March
Check #7	$375 (1/2 half of rent)	
Check #8	$750	April

Check #9	$375 (1/2 half of rent)	
Check #10	$750	May
Check #11	$375 (1/2 half of rent)	
Check #12	$750	June
Check #13	$375 (1/2 half of rent)	
Check #14	$750	July
Check #15	$375 (1/2 half of rent)	
Check #16	$750	August
Check #17	$375 (1/2 half of rent)	
Check #18	$750	September
Check #19	$375 (1/2 half of rent)	
Check #20	$750	October
Check #21	$375 (1/2 half of rent)	
Check #22	$750	November
Check #23	$375 (1/2 half of rent)	
Check #24	$750	December
Check #25	$375	
Check #26	$750	Payment #13 *WooHoo*

Staying Motivated

This has been a challenge for me. I have been much more enthusiastic than other times. My saving grace has been having a circle of people around me that are also working on being coming debt free and YouTube. I have watched hours of videos of people detailing their Debt Free struggles. Followed by them yelling at the top of their lungs – *"I'm Debt Free*!!!" This has helped me to feel less secluded and it also has given me motivation that if they could do it, I could do the same.

It is also possible to also take classes online such as a free one offered by BYU: http://personalfinance.byu.edu/content/moneywise-financial-workshops

Use visuals. Create charts that show your progress. Post them in places that you can easily see them. On a door, the refrigerator, etc. If you are not artistic, there are downloadable charts available at: http://debtfreecharts.blogspot.com/p/all-charts.html

Teaching Your Children

Remember that you are your children's first teacher and you have the opportunity to give your children a head start. Think about it, how many times have I mentioned my father in this book? Anyway, many people are not taught proper money management, but your children are fortunate that you have made the decision to make a paradigm shift. You can teach your children financial literacy using with your actions and with games and through watching videos.

Family Game Night
Not only do these Board games that teach money skills, in the long run they can also save you money as you are not going out on expensive outings with the children:

Cashflow 101
Monopoly
Payday
The Game Of Life
Charge Large
Act Your Wage
Finance
Jade
Careers
Awesome Island
The farming game
Money Bags
The Allowance Game

Videos:
This cartoon series is by far the best video collection for children that I have ever seen.

https://www.youtube.com/user/CashVilleKidz

The End

Overview of steps to become debt free

- Decide that you want to become debt free and that you are willing to sacrifice to make it happen.

- Look debt in the face. Compile a list of ALL of your debts, from MasterCard to that $20 that you borrowed from your Grandmother

- Stop Creating MORE debt

- Create a spending plan (A Budget)

- Establish a Rainy-Day Fund (Emergency Fund)

- Use only CASH and pay bills on time

- Increase Your Income

- Be Consistent

Tracking Your Debt Free Journey

Name	Initial Bill	Current Bill	Settlement Amount	Amount Saved
Mortgage 1				
Mortgage 2				
Car Payment 1				
Car Payment 2				
Student Loan				
Credit Card 1				
Credit Card 2				
Judgment 1				
Judgment 2				
Hospital Bill				
Payday Loan				

Acknowledgements

I have been blessed to write a few books and thus far, this has been the hardest. Probably because I have been staring in the mirror the entire time. (smile) I am so thankful for the following people that have helped me along the way:

Thank you, Rasheed L. Muhammad, for the challenge.

When people really LOVE and BELIEVE in you, they will give you your very own bedroom in their home, just so that you can come visit them and write in silence. They will also remind you, "That's Your Room." Thank you, Cousin, Geralean Evans and my EWF homegirl LaRita Simon for giving me my very own rooms. (smile)

Teammates ~ Cheerleaders ~ Accountability Partners:
Giselle Muhammad for being a sounding board. Phyillis Muhammad for being a motivator and example. James Samuel for always saying – "You can do it Cuzzzzz". Maricea Muhammad for being an accountability partner and extremely transparent. Linda Muhammad for being a mentor and a cheerleader. Karen J. Wynn you still must admit … it was a gorgeous handbag – but you were right.

Thank you, Reggie C. Young, for your money advice. Khallada F. Mita for sharing your student loan stories and money visions. Tiyika Tonge-Mason, for growing my debt paying game with so many impelling opportunities.

Thank You ~ Thank You ~ Thank You to my Father, Bobby Joe Harris. Even though he is not physically here to read this, I must thank him for what he taught me through practical application and conversations. Because of this learning, I am able to teach others.

****

Assets:
Land – Artwork – Checking Account – Jewelry & Furs – Mutual Funds
Liabilities:
Jordan Sneakers – Credit Cards – House – BMW 535i – Student Loans

Made in the USA
Coppell, TX
10 January 2020